PERSPECTIVE

THE WAY YOU SEE

SWAIKA

BlueRose ONE.com
Stories Matter
NewDelhi • London

BLUEROSE PUBLISHERS
India | U.K.

BlueRose ONE.com
Stories Matter
NewDelhi • London

For permissions requests or inquiries regarding this publication, please contact:

BLUEROSE PUBLISHERS
www.BlueRoseONE.com
info@bluerosepublishers.com
+91 8882 898 898
+4407342408967

ISBN: 978-93-6261-922-8

Cover design: Tahira
Typesetting: Tanya Raj Upadhyay

First Edition: May 2024

To my mamma and babai, who never stopped believing in me.

Table of Contents

Introduction

The complex story of human behaviour is revealed in a world where the idea of perfect self-awareness and the certainty of social correctness are valued highly. Together, we will investigate the mystery that contradicts these widely accepted notions as we navigate the pathways of literacy, education, and society.

There is a contradiction in the field of literacy and education. A culture is more likely to claim that its understanding of the universe is true the more educated and literate it grows. Unquestionably a lighthouse of enlightenment, education endows people with information and the capacity for critical thought. But it also breeds a kind of conceit that makes one oblivious to the immensity of the unknown. Behind the curtain of presumptive certainty, the complex fabric of society, woven with a variety of viewpoints and experiences, is frequently hidden.

The three components of the human psyche—the brain, heart, and mind—create a dynamic interaction between feelings, reason, and intuition. Although we may believe that our conscious thought processes allow us to know ourselves, the subconscious mind is a treasure trove of uncharted territory. In addition to serving as outward indicators of success, dreams, ambitions, and accomplishments also serve as windows into the maze-like network of desires and aspirations hidden deep within our subconscious. Navigating this complex terrain and realising the impact of both conscious and subconscious factors on our perceptions and choices are essential to understanding who we are.

Strong mentality and determination are frequently seen as the cornerstones of confidence and social appropriateness. Nevertheless, the idea of unwavering power is called into question by the intricacy of the human intellect. Numerous circumstances might affect mental health, thus maintaining a careful balance and showing compassion are necessary. When the reality of mental health issues is faced, the mask of social correctness falls apart, underscoring the importance of empathy and a complex understanding of human nature.

The global difficulties of overpopulation and underemployment raise doubt on the claimed soundness of society systems. As civilizations face the impacts of their own prosperity, the gap between expectations and reality grows. The notion that civilizations can clearly grasp and manage their problems is challenged by these complex, interwoven difficulties, prompting a collective rethinking of conventional wisdom.

Exploring the subconscious mind exposes an abundance of untapped potential and power. The subconscious, which is sometimes disregarded in the pursuit of conscious knowledge, contains the secret to unleashing creativity, resilience, and transformation. Recognising the power of the subconscious challenges the notion that we fully understand ourselves, promoting a deeper examination of the layers that affect our thoughts and actions.

The debate over methods for understanding the human mind between psychology and pseudosciences continues. While psychology seeks evidence-based insights into human behaviour, pseudosciences frequently present basic, enticing tales. Society's proclivity for the soothing simplicity of pseudosciences reveals a vulnerability in the collective psyche, highlighting the limitations in our ability to distinguish between actual insight and illusory certainty.

As we navigate the intricate details of human existence, it becomes evident that the truths we hold close are frequently far from absolute. The journey to self-awareness and societal knowledge is an ongoing exploration of the unknown, necessitating humility, curiosity, and a willingness to examine the fundamental roots of our ideas. Only by accepting the complexities of the human experience can we expect to unlock the secrets that lay beyond the surface of our assumptions and discover a deeper truth about ourselves and the society we live in. So, let us go into much more detail to ensure that we understand each of these completely.

Literate, Educated and Society

Literacy and education are two of the most important cornerstones of human development and society progress. This paper investigates the complex relationship between literacy and education, as well as their overall impact on society. We investigate the importance of literacy, the complex role of education, and how both contribute to a thriving society.

The terms "literate" and "educated" are related but separate, referring to different characteristics of a person's knowledge and abilities. Here are the main distinctions between the two:

1. Literate:

The capacity to read and write is referred to as literacy. A literate individual is capable of comprehending and generating written language, which is a necessary skill for communication and information access. Literacy is frequently connected with basic or effective reading and writing abilities. It does not always imply a comprehensive or deep understanding of a variety of subjects.

• Literacy is often measured via standardised exams or self-reported ability to read and write in a given language.

2. Educated:

Education is a broader notion that includes not only reading and writing but also the acquisition of knowledge, skills, and intellectual development through formal or informal means. A well-educated person has gone through an organised learning process that may have included schooling, college or university education, vocational training, and self-directed study. This procedure often covers a broad range of topics and areas of knowledge.

• Critical thinking, problem solving, and the capacity to apply knowledge to real-world circumstances are all part of education. It extends beyond basic literacy to a more in-depth study of numerous areas such as mathematics, physics, history, and the arts.

• Being educated entails a higher level of intellectual and cognitive growth than simply being literate.

In brief, literacy is the fundamental capacity to read and write, but education is a larger term that encompasses formal and informal learning, intellectual development, and the acquisition of knowledge and skills across multiple domains. A well-educated person is usually literate, but a literate person is not always well-educated in the wide sense.

What is Literacy?

Literacy is a multidimensional notion that encompasses much more than the ability to read and write. Literacy is defined as the capacity to comprehend, interpret, and employ written language effectively. It is a fundamental talent that allows people to interact with their surroundings, process information, and communicate ideas. Let's break down the essential elements of literacy:

1. Reading Literacy

When addressing literacy, reading literacy is frequently the first thing that comes to mind. It includes the capacity to comprehend written texts, such as books, newspapers, websites, or any other type of written content. A literate individual can read and understand written words, phrases, and paragraphs. This ability is essential for acquiring knowledge, learning, and remaining informed about the world.

2. Writing Literacy

Writing literacy is the inverse of reading literacy. It entails the ability to express thoughts, ideas, and facts in writing. Personal expression, communication, and documentation all require this competence. A literate individual is capable of writing intelligible and effective messages, whether they are letters, essays, reports, or emails.

3. Comprehension

Literacy extends beyond the ability to read and write to include comprehension. A literate person can comprehend what they read, distinguish important concepts, draw inferences, and critically assess material. Understanding is essential for making informed judgements, critical thinking, and participating in discussions.

4. Critical Thinking

Literacy and critical thinking skills are inextricably linked. A literate individual can assess the dependability and authenticity of written material and create their own opinions. In today's digital age, where disinformation and biased content are common, critical thinking is vital for interpreting the large amount of information available.

5. Digital Literacy

Literacy in the modern world extends to the digital sphere. The capacity to use digital devices, browse the internet, and interact with digital content is referred to as digital literacy. In the digital age, this type of literacy is becoming increasingly vital for job, communication, and information access.

6. Information Literacy

Information literacy is a subset of literacy that focuses on the capacity to successfully find, assess, and use information. It entails abilities such as performing research, citing sources, and distinguishing between credible and untrustworthy information sources. Information literacy is critical in an age of information overload.

7. Media Literacy

The ability to critically analyse and comprehend various forms of media, such as television, radio, newspapers, and digital media, is referred to as media literacy. A literate person can decipher media messages, identify bias, and interpret the impact of media on society and culture.

8. Cultural Literacy

Understanding one's own and other societies' cultures, traditions, and values is a necessary component of cultural literacy. It makes it possible for people to appreciate literature and the arts, interact with others from different cultural backgrounds, and promote intercultural understanding.

9. Numeracy

Although numeracy is not a traditional component of literacy, it is frequently regarded as a necessary auxiliary skill. Understanding, utilising, and interpreting numerical data is the essence of numeracy, which is essential for everyday problem-solving, scientific literacy, and financial literacy.

In conclusion, having a wide range of skills in reading, writing, understanding, critical thinking, digital literacy, information literacy, media literacy, and cultural literacy is what it means to be literate. These abilities are essential for involvement in the modern world, education, personal growth, and communication. The skill of literacy is dynamic and ever-changing, adjusting to the ever-shifting technological and informational environment. It provides people the ability to effectively and confidently navigate this complicated world.

Understanding Literacy

The definition of literacy has expanded over time to include a wide range of abilities and competencies. It is a complex and dynamic notion. The capacity to read and write has historically been the definition of literacy, however in the modern world, this definition is insufficient. These days, being literate involves more than just reading and writing; it also involves understanding, assessing, and applying many kinds of information and communication in productive ways. We will examine the changing meaning of literacy and the range of aspects it includes in this section.

Traditional Literacy

The fundamental definition of traditional literacy is the capacity to read and write in a language, usually one's mother tongue. This calls for the ability to read and comprehend written symbols, such as characters, letters, or hieroglyphs, as well as the ability to put together cohesive written compositions. A basic ability that facilitates education, communication, and personal growth is traditional literacy. People wouldn't be able to read written material, take part in written conversations, or do many other things in modern life without it.

Beyond Reading and Writing

Today's definition of literacy extends beyond proficiency in writing and reading. It involves the capacity to comprehend, evaluate, and decipher textual material. This is frequently called "comprehensive literacy" or "functional literacy." A person with extensive literacy can:

1. **Comprehend Texts:** They are able to decipher written material, ranging from straightforward stories to intricate academic works.

2. **Critically Evaluate Information:** They are able to distinguish between accurate and false information by evaluating the reliability and calibre of sources.

3. **Communicate Effectively:** They are able to express their ideas, opinions, and thoughts in writing, which makes communication understandable and significant.

Multiple Literacies

Different forms of literacy have arisen in the digital age, reflecting the range of skills required to traverse an information world that is evolving quickly. A few of these consist of:

1. **Digital literacy:** This includes having the necessary skills to efficiently use digital tools, software, and the internet. Digital literacy encompasses knowledge of internet security and privacy as well as abilities like email communication and online research.

2. **Information Literacy:** Finding, assessing, and using information from a variety of sources—including the internet, databases, and libraries—is the essence of information literacy. It entails distinguishing reliable information from skewed or fraudulent data.

3. **Media Literacy:** The study of media content, including print, broadcast, and digital media, critically is the main goal of media literacy. It entails figuring out how media messages are put together, deciphering what they mean, and identifying media bias.

4. **Visual Literacy:** The capacity to comprehend and analyse visual data, such as pictures, graphs, charts, and infographics, is known as visual literacy. In a world where visual communication is ubiquitous, it is important.

Cultural Literacy

Another kind of literacy is cultural literacy, which is concerned with an individual's comprehension of the cultural allusions and symbols present in their community or in a particular cultural setting. This covers an understanding of literature, art, history, and customs. People that possess cultural literacy are more equipped to interact within their community, comprehend cultural allusions, and participate more completely in their culture.

Global Literacy

Global literacy has become increasingly important as the globe grows more interconnected. Understanding international issues and cultures as well as having the ability to communicate across cultural boundaries are requirements for this type of literacy. In addition to promoting greater empathy and collaboration, global literacy helps people negotiate the complexity of our increasingly interconnected world.

Summing-up

To sum up, literacy has developed well beyond the conventional meaning of writing and reading. These days, it includes a wide range of abilities and proficiencies, such as media literacy, cultural literacy, information literacy, and digital literacy. The idea of literacy keeps growing as our society gets more intricate and linked. In the twenty-first century, being literate is more than just being able to read and write; it also involves possessing a broad variety of abilities that allow people to prosper in a digital, globalised, information-rich environment. The concept of literacy is dynamic and ever-changing, reflecting the ways in which communication and the transmission of knowledge are altering and adjusting to the demands of modern society.

Traditional literacy (verbosely)

The fundamental capacity to read and write in a language, usually one's native tongue, is traditional literacy, sometimes known as basic literacy. It requires the ability to create coherent written texts as well as the basic skills of reading and comprehending written symbols, which can be characters, letters, or hieroglyphs. A basic ability that facilitates education, communication, and personal growth is traditional literacy. It makes it possible for people to interact with many facets of contemporary life, read written material, and take part in written debate.

Important elements of traditional literacy consist of:

1. Reading: The capacity to decode and comprehend written words. Recognising letters, words, and sentences, as well as comprehending the substance of written texts, are all part of this.

2. Writing: The ability to write intelligible written documents ranging from simple lines to complex essays or reports. Grammar, syntax, and vocabulary are all part of it.

Traditional literacy is frequently required as a foundation for subsequent education and personal growth. It is the entryway to obtaining and comprehending written information, whether in the form of books, newspapers, educational materials, or digital content. Individuals who lack traditional literacy may struggle to navigate the modern world, where written communication is prevalent in many parts of life, including school, employment, and civic engagement.

While traditional literacy is a vital basic skill, in today's information age, it is frequently viewed as merely one component of a broader set of literacy abilities that includes digital literacy, information literacy, media literacy, and more. These additional literacies reflect the wide range of abilities required to flourish in a fast-changing, digitally connected world.

Traditional literacy and education are connected ideas, but their scope and aim are distinct. The following are the fundamental distinctions between traditional literacy and education:

1. Definition:

• Traditional literacy refers to the fundamental capacity to read and write in a language. It emphasises on the fundamental skills of recognising and comprehending written symbols as well as writing coherently. Traditional literacy is a fundamental ability that allows people to interact with written information and communicate in writing.

• Education: Education refers to the overall process of learning knowledge, skills, values, and attitudes. It involves both official learning (attending schools, colleges, and universities) and informal learning (from diverse life experiences). Education strives to promote intellectual, social, and personal development and might include disciplines and skills other than standard literacy.

2. Scope:

• Traditional Literacy: Traditional literacy is primarily concerned with reading and writing abilities. It is a subset of education that focuses on a specific set of skills connected to written communication.

• Education: Education is a multidimensional process that extends beyond literacy. It encompasses a wide range of subjects, disciplines, and fields of knowledge, including mathematics, science, history, art, and others. Education also includes the development of social and interpersonal skills, critical thinking, problem solving, and moral and ethical values.

3.Purpose:

• Traditional Literacy: The basic goal of traditional literacy is to enable people to read and write efficiently. It is a fundamental ability that allows for easier access to information, communication, and basic textual interactions. Traditional literacy is frequently viewed as a means to an end, with the ultimate goal of being able to function in a literate society.

• Education: Education serves a greater purpose, including personal and intellectual development, the acquisition of a diverse variety of knowledge and skills, and the development of critical thinking and problem-solving ability. Education is intended to prepare students for numerous elements of life, such as careers, citizenship, and personal development.

4.Duration:

• Traditional Literacy: Traditional literacy can be acquired rather fast, often in a person's early years of life. It is commonly regarded as a core ability learned during primary school.

• Education is a lifetime process that can extend far beyond the early years of schooling. It includes both official education in schools and colleges, as well as lifelong learning.

5.Context:

• Traditional Literacy: Traditional literacy is a skill that is required for individuals to function in a literate culture. It is a foundation upon which other types of education can be built.

• Education: Education can take place in a variety of formal and informal settings, including the family, community, workplace, and official educational institutions. It adjusts to various stages of life and learning situations.

In summary, traditional literacy, which focuses on the ability to read and write, is a core component of education. In contrast, education is a bigger and more thorough process that includes a wide range of information and skills, personal and intellectual development, and lifelong learning. While conventional literacy is an important component of education, education encompasses a broader range of individual development and societal needs.

Formal and Informal Learning

Formal and informal learning are two unique approaches to acquire knowledge and skills. They are distinct in terms of structure, context, and goal. Here's a breakdown of each:

Formal Education:

1. Structure and Setting: Formal learning is structured and organised, and it often occurs within an institution or a formal educational setting. Schools, colleges, universities, vocational training centres, and corporate training programmes are examples of this. Formal learning includes a curriculum, learning objectives, and a term of study.

2. Intention: Formal learning is deliberate and frequently results in recognised certificates or certifications. Formal learning's major purpose is to equip individuals with an organised and methodical approach to acquiring knowledge and skills. It is intended to meet certain academic standards and requirements.

3. Instructors: In formal learning, trained instructors or teachers deliver content and assess learners' progress. Exams, assignments, and grades are examples of recognised techniques of evaluation and assessment.

4. Examples: Attending school to acquire a degree, enrolling in a professional certification programme, or participating in workplace training programmes sponsored by an employer are all examples of formal learning.

Informal Learning:

1. Structure and Setting: Informal learning is unstructured and occurs naturally in everyday life. There is no structured curriculum or syllabus, and there are no defined learning objectives. Informal learning can occur anywhere, including the family, business, or community.

2. Intention: Informal learning is frequently inadvertent. It happens spontaneously as people engage in various activities and interact with their surroundings. Personal curiosity and the desire to address real-world problems motivate it.

3. Instructors: In most cases, informal learning does not include formal instructors or teachers. Individuals instead learn by personal experience, trial & error, observation, and interaction with others. Informal learning frequently involves learning from peers, mentors, or through self-directed discovery.

4. Examples: Informal learning includes experimenting with recipes at home, gaining computer skills through self-exploration and online courses, and learning about a foreign culture by living and interacting with individuals from that society.

Key Distinctions:

1. Structure: Formal learning is structured and follows a specific curriculum, whereas informal learning is unstructured and occurs organically.

2. Setting: Formal learning normally takes place in educational facilities, although informal learning can take place anywhere.

3. Intention: Formal learning is deliberate and goal-oriented, whereas informal learning is typically haphazard and driven by personal interest or immediate requirements.

4. Instructors: While formal learning frequently requires qualified teachers, informal learning is based on self-directed learning, observation, and interaction with others.

It's worth noting that both formal and informal learning have advantages and are useful in different settings. Formal learning is necessary for providing an organised and thorough education, whereas informal learning allows individuals to continuously adapt and acquire knowledge throughout their lives, typically in reaction to changing environmental needs. To achieve their educational and personal development needs, many people use a blend of formal and informal learning.

Literacy, education, and one's interaction with society are all intertwined and play important roles in defining the evolution and development of communities. Let's look at each of these concepts and how they interact with society:

Literate:

Definition of Literacy : Literacy is defined as the capacity to read and write in a language, often one's native tongue. It comprises the ability to recognise written symbols, decode words, comprehend written materials, and write coherently. However, literacy comprises the ability to grasp and critically evaluate many forms of information and communication in a larger sense.

Role in Society:

1. Access to Knowledge: Literacy serves as a gateway to knowledge and information. It enables people to read books, newspapers, research articles, and digital content in order to stay informed and broaden their horizons.

2. Communication: Effective communication requires literacy. It enables people to write down their thoughts, ideas, and opinions, allowing meaningful connections and engagement with society.

3. Civic Participation: Literate people are more prepared to participate in civic life. They can vote, understand government programmes, and participate in the political process.

4. Employment: Literacy is frequently required for a wide range of employment and career prospects. It improves an individual's employability and adaptability to changing work markets.

5. Personal Development: Literacy promotes personal development by encouraging critical thinking, problem solving, and lifelong learning. It fosters intellectual development and self-expression.

6. Preservation of Culture: Literacy helps to preserve cultural heritage through the written word. It enables communities to record their history, customs, and values.

Educated:

Definition of Education: A thorough process that comprises structured learning experiences aimed at obtaining knowledge, skills, and values is defined as education. It extends beyond literacy to include critical thinking, problem solving, and practical application of knowledge.

Role in Society:

1. **Economic Development:** Education provides people with the knowledge and skills they need to work. It promotes entrepreneurship, innovation, and economic progress.

2. **Social Mobility:** Education is a tool for social mobility since it allows people to enhance their socioeconomic standing. It has the potential to break the cycle of poverty and open doors to greater opportunities.

3. **Cultural Understanding:** Education fosters cultural understanding and tolerance by exposing people to other points of view and worldviews. It helps to create a more informed and compassionate society.

4. **Problem Solving:** Well-educated people are better able to face complicated societal difficulties and make sound decisions. Education fosters critical thinking and analytical abilities.

5. **Scientific and Technological Advancement:** Scientific and technological breakthroughs are driven by education, resulting in innovations that benefit society as a whole.

6. **Social Cohesiveness:** Education can promote social cohesiveness by instilling shared ideals, civic responsibility, and a sense of belonging.

Society:

The aggregate body of humans who are interconnected and share a common culture, values, and institutions is referred to as society. In terms of literacy and education:

1. Literacy and Education as Social Foundations: Literacy and education are critical pillars of a healthy, progressing society. They contribute to a community's intellectual, economic, and social development.

2. Societal Advancement: Literacy and education are important contributors to societal advancement. They result in better healthcare, lower poverty, greater access to information, and stronger problem-solving ability.

3. Inequalities: Inequalities can arise as a result of societal imbalances in literacy and education. It is critical to address these gaps in order to promote social justice and inclusivity.

4. Cultural Heritage: Literacy and education play an important role in the preservation and transmission of cultural heritage and customs from one generation to the next.

5. Economic Growth: A well-educated and literate populace is an important resource for economic growth and prosperity. It attracts investments, boosts innovation, and develops a competent workforce.

Literate Society: A literate society is one in which a considerable proportion of the population can read and write. Literacy refers to the ability to recognise and comprehend written language in this context. It is a key talent that enables people to decode written symbols, comprehend written words, and write coherent written documents.

Individuals in a literate society have the ability to communicate successfully through written language. They can read books, newspapers, web content, and other written materials. This fundamental ability is critical for personal development because it allows people to engage in self-directed learning, express themselves in writing, and participate in basic written communication.

Educated Society: An educated society is one that goes beyond mere literacy. It means that a sizable proportion of the population has received formal education, gaining not only the ability to read and write but also a broader knowledge base and a diverse range of skills. Education includes areas such as mathematics and physics, as well as humanities, social studies, and the arts.

Individuals in an educated society have had the opportunity to participate in structured learning through educational institutions such as schools, colleges, and universities. They have perfected skills in critical thinking, problem solving, and specialised fields of study, in addition to superior reading. Education gives people the ability to analyse information, use knowledge, and make sound judgements.

Interplay: While literacy is a prerequisite for education, the two notions are inextricably linked. Education is the systematic process by which people gain advanced literacy skills and a broad knowledge foundation. Literacy is, in essence, a fundamental component of education because it is the foundation upon which the rest of the educational experience is formed.

A literate society creates the circumstances for individuals to participate in the educational process. Individuals who have mastered basic literacy might then start on a formal education path to further expand their skills and knowledge. Education, in turn, improves and broadens their literacy abilities. Literacy and education are both critical for developing knowledgeable, active, and involved individuals who contribute to society's prosperity, inclusivity, and cultural vibrancy.

In brief, literacy and education are important factors of an individual's contributions to society and personal well-being. A literate and educated populace is essential for society development, as it promotes economic growth, cultural preservation, and social progress. Addressing literacy and education difficulties is critical for establishing a more equal and successful society.

In general, an educated person is unlikely to be fully illiterate. Literacy skills, which are essential for communication and learning, are often taught in schools. However, there may be some exceptions or unusual cases in which a person has a formal education and extensive expertise in numerous subjects but still suffers with basic literacy. Here are a few examples of how this could happen:

1. Learning difficulties: Some people have unique learning difficulties, such as dyslexia, which makes learning and applying basic reading and writing skills difficult. These individuals may, nevertheless, succeed in other areas of schooling.

2. Late Bloomers: In some situations, people may have had early educational hurdles or disruptions, such as restricted access to quality education, and only learn fundamental literacy skills later in life, even after receiving higher schooling.

3. Non-Native Language Use: Individuals who receive their education in a language other than their native language may struggle with literacy in that language. This is something that can happen in multilingual or multinational educational contexts.

4. Limited Exposure: If a well-educated individual has mostly worked in non-literacy-dependent industries or has had limited practical use of reading and writing in their everyday life or profession, their literacy skills may deteriorate with time.

While there are exceptions, it is critical to recognise that literacy is a core ability in most formal education systems, and educated individuals are expected to have gained at least basic literacy abilities along their educational journey. Advanced education frequently necessitates not only good literacy abilities but also knowledge of a variety of disciplines and areas of specialisation.

It is quite rare for an educated individual to be illiterate. Literacy skills are a core component of education, which is normally given through official institutions such as schools, colleges, and universities. Individuals learn to read and write as part of their basic education in most educational systems.

However, in some extraordinary and rare instances, an educated individual may be illiterate. Among these scenarios are:

1. Learning difficulties: Even while enrolled in formal schooling, certain people with specific learning difficulties may struggle to acquire reading skills. Reading and writing skills might be hampered by learning difficulties.

2. Late-Onset Education: Individuals who did not obtain formal education during their early years may seek education later in life in some instances. They may gain knowledge in a variety of disciplines, but they may not achieve full literacy.

3. Immigrants and Refugees: Even if they have extensive education in their native language, individuals who have relocated to a new nation and entered an educational system with a different language or writing system may suffer initial literacy issues.

4. Health Disorders: Certain health disorders or traumatic experiences can have an impact on a person's cognitive capacities, including literacy skills.

5. Cultural or Religious Isolation: Individuals in particularly remote or insular societies may have restricted access to formal education, resulting in some educated members who are less adept in reading and writing.

It is essential to reiterate that such occurrences are anomalies, and in most circumstances, education involves literacy as a core ability. Being educated often means not simply increased literacy abilities, but also a broader knowledge base and the capacity to think critically and solve problems.

Differences Between Literacy and Education

While literacy and education share certain common goals, they differ in several fundamental ways:

Nature and Range

• **Literacy:** Literacy is largely concerned with reading and writing abilities. It entails being able to decipher written symbols, recognise letters and words, and comprehend written materials. It has a smaller scope, focused on language abilities.

• **Education:** Education encompasses a vast range of subjects, knowledge domains, and competencies. It encompasses critical thinking, problem solving, and the acquisition of information and abilities in a variety of subjects.

Objectives and Outcomes

• **Literacy:** Literacy's major purpose is to enable people to read, write, and communicate effectively in written language. Improved communication, access to written information, and basic written skill are among the outcomes.

• **Education:** Education goals include not simply reading but also the acquisition of a broad knowledge foundation, specialised skills, critical thinking, and problem-solving ability. Education seeks to prepare students for personal and professional success while also encouraging intellectual development.

Informal vs. Formal

• **Literacy:** Although literacy can be gained informally through self-guided reading and writing activities, it is frequently taught professionally in educational settings.

• **Education:** It consists of both formal and informal components. Informal education occurs through self-directed learning and everyday life experiences, whereas formal education occurs within established institutions.

Lifelong Education

- **Literacy:** Once learned, literacy skills are often lifelong assets. Literacy, on the other hand, does not inherently foster lifelong learning because it concentrates on reading and writing ability.

- **Education:** Education stresses the value of lifelong learning. It promotes people to constantly learn new things, adapt to changing situations, and engage in personal and professional development.

The Interplay of Literacy and Education

While the breadth and nature of literacy and education varies, they are inextricably linked and frequently compliment one other. The following summarises the link between literacy and education:

- **Literacy as a Foundation for Education:** Literacy serves as the foundation for formal education. Individuals must first gain fundamental literacy skills before they may participate in formal education. Understanding texts, following instructions, and engaging in educational activities all require literacy. It acts as a gateway to education.

- **Education's Contribution to Literacy:** Education not only conveys advanced knowledge but also refines and expands literacy skills. Literacy skills are developed in educational environments to help pupils to access and process information in a variety of subjects. Education strengthens and improves literacy, making it a more adaptable and powerful tool for students.

Impact on Individuals

The Impact of Literacy

Literacy has a profound effect on people, influencing many parts of their lives:

- **Communication and Expression:** Literacy helps people to successfully communicate through written language. It enables people to express their thoughts, ideas, and feelings, resulting in more meaningful connections with others.

- **Access to Information:** Literacy gives people access to a variety of written information. It enables people to stay informed, conduct research, and investigate a wide range of issues.

- **Personal Development:** Literacy can be used to help with personal development and enrichment. It allows people to pursue self-directed learning, explore their interests, and gain access to a massive store of written knowledge.

- **Economic Opportunities:** Strong literacy skills improve people's employability. Because many occupations and careers demand reading, writing, and computer ability, literate people are more appealing to employers.

The Transformative Power of Education

Individuals are transformed by education, which has a broader scope and goals:

- **Expertise and knowledge:** Education provides individuals with a broad knowledge base as well as specialised expertise in their chosen disciplines. This information broadens their comprehension of the world and certain topics.

- **Critical Thinking and Problem Solving:** Education encourages critical thinking, analytical talents, and problem-solving capabilities. Individuals learn to methodically tackle complex topics and make informed conclusions.

- **Career Advancement:** Education provides opportunities for higher-paying jobs and career advancement. It equips individuals with sought-after specialised skills and certificates.

- **Innovation and Research:** Educational institutions act as innovation and research hubs, propelling breakthroughs in a variety of sectors. Through research, innovation, and technological growth, education drives progress.

- **Social Mobility:** Education is a powerful tool for social mobility, enabling people to overcome socioeconomic barriers and improve their lives. It breaks poverty and disadvantageous cycles.

Disparities and Obstacles

While reading and education both provide various benefits, there are several obstacles and discrepancies that must be addressed:

Literacy Availability

- **Gender gaps:** Gender gaps in literacy exist in many parts of the world, with women having limited access to educational opportunities and literacy programmes.

• **Geographic Disparities:** Because rural and distant communities frequently have limited access to quality education and literacy resources, literacy rates differ.

• **Socio-Economic Disparities:** Disparities in access to education and literacy can be caused by socio-economic variables. Individuals from low-income families may suffer educational and literacy development difficulties.

Disparities in Education

• **Education Quality:** There are disparities in educational quality, with some educational institutions providing better resources and opportunities than others.

• **Access to Higher Education:** Some persons' access to higher education may be limited, particularly owing to financial restrictions, resulting in discrepancies in advanced educational attainment.

• **Digital Divide:** In the digital age, gaps in access to online education and digital literacy can affect marginalised populations.

Aspect	Literacy	Education
Definition	The ability to read and write.	A comprehensive process of learning that includes knowledge, skills, and competencies.
Focus	Primarily on reading and writing.	Encompasses a broad range of subjects, skills, and competencies.
Scope	Fundamental and basic.	Comprehensive and holistic.
Formality	Informal or formal.	Formal within organized institutions.

Skills Acquired	Reading, writing, basic comprehension.	Critical thinking, problem-solving, specialized knowledge.
Setting	Can be acquired anywhere.	Occurs within formal educational institutions.
Role in Communication	Facilitates basic written communication.	Enables complex discourse and comprehensive understanding.
Economic Implications	Limited economic impact.	Often leads to better job prospects and higher earning potential.
Cultural and Historical Role	Preserves and transmits culture and heritage through reading and writing.	Fosters a deeper understanding of culture and history.
Access to Information	Provides limited access to information.	Facilitates efficient access to a wide range of knowledge.
Certification or Credentials	Generally no formal certification.	Results in recognized degrees, diplomas, or certifications.

Brain, Heart and Mind

The terms "brain," "heart," and "mind" are frequently used to refer to many parts of human experience and functioning, both literally and metaphorically. Here's a quick rundown of what each of these phrases might mean:

1. Brain: The brain is the physical organ in the human body that processes information, controls bodily activities, and generates thoughts and emotions. It is the nerve system's centre and is involved in many cognitive activities such as thinking, remembering, and problem solving. It is also in charge of essential bodily activities such as breathing, heart rate, and body temperature.

2. Heart: A literal definition of the heart is a muscular organ that pumps blood throughout the circulatory system, supplying oxygen and nutrition to the body's tissues. It is required for life to exist. The "heart" is frequently associated with emotions, feelings, and the seat of one's affections in a metaphorical sense. When people talk about "following their heart" or having a "kind heart," they are referring to their emotional and sensitive selves.

3. Mind: The mind is a more abstract and difficult notion to grasp. Cognitive processes, consciousness, thoughts, beliefs, perceptions, and emotions are all included. It is frequently regarded as the seat of cognition and consciousness. The mind enables us to think, reason, feel emotions, and construct subjective world experiences and interpretations. It is strongly tied to the brain but does not stop there; it also includes the subjective experience of mental life.

Now, let's look at the metaphorical aspect.

The terms "brain," "heart," and "mind" are frequently used metaphorically to express various aspects of human experience, character, and decision-making. Here's one example of how they're widely used metaphorically:

1. Brain: The "brain" is frequently connected with logic, reasoning, and analytical thinking in a metaphorical sense. When someone is said to be using their "brain," it implies that they make decisions based on facts, evidence, and deliberate thought. It can also symbolise problem-solving abilities and intelligence. For instance, "He used his brain to solve the complex puzzle."

2. Heart: The "heart" metaphorically denotes emotions, feelings, and empathy. It is frequently used to characterise decisions or behaviours motivated by love, compassion, or personal ideals. For example, when someone says, "I followed my heart," they are referring to a decision they made based on their sentiments and what they actually care about, even if it was not the most reasonable one.

3. Mind: In a metaphorical sense, the "mind" includes both cognitive and emotional qualities. It can relate to both reasonable reasoning and deep thought. When someone is stated to have a "strong mind," it implies that they are intellectually capable as well as emotionally resilient. The concept of "mind" can also refer to consciousness and self-awareness. he said, "He has a brilliant mind, but he also understands the human condition."

Let us comprehend in a more elaborated manner.

The Brain

The "brain" is a symbol of cognitive prowess, analytical thinking, and intellectual capacity. This metaphorical portrayal of the brain digs into the complicated interaction of reason, strategy, and problem-solving within the human experience. It offers a glimpse into the complex tapestry of human cognition and the relevance of the brain as a metaphorical powerhouse.

1. The Brain as the Citadel of Reason

One of the most common metaphors for the brain is that it is the citadel of reason. When we attribute a decision or action to the "brain," we evoke images of meticulous calculation and a reliance on analytical thinking. In this context, the brain represents the repository of facts, evidence, and well-considered judgement. Decisions that are "from the brain" are generally seen as systematic and data-driven, anchored by a dedication to critical analysis and objective judgement.

Metaphorically, the brain serves as a fortress of logic, capable of marshalling arguments, assessing evidence, and reaching well-founded judgements. It is related with intellectual prowess and the ability to distinguish between truth and untruth, fact and fiction. When we engage in serious reflection, analytical problem-solving, and strategic planning, we put on the metaphorical "thinking cap." It's a call to use our cognitive abilities, to put our intellectual resources to use, and to tackle complex problems with a clear, rational perspective.

2. The Brain as a Knowledge of Repository

The brain is frequently described metaphorically as a repository of knowledge as well as experience. It is where we keep knowledge, information, and wisdom accumulated throughout time. When we remark that someone "has a lot on their mind," we are referring to the brain's accumulation of thoughts and memories. The metaphorical "brain library" contains a large amount of information gained via education, life experiences, and continual learning.

The brain is compared to a massive encyclopaedia or a treasure trove of ideas in this metaphorical setting. It signifies an individual's lifetime accumulation of communal wisdom and information. People frequently seek to "exercise their brain" in order to keep this repository of knowledge sharp and current. Engaging in intellectual pursuits, reading, and seeking out new experiences are all methods to build and extend the brain's metaphorical library.

3. The Brain as a Source of Creativity and Innovation

The metaphorical representation of the brain includes more than just pure reason and analytical thought; it also includes creativity and innovation. The brain is a source of creative ideas and artistic expression. The brain can be viewed metaphorically as the birthplace of innovation, a space where new ideas, inventions, and artistic achievements are conceived.

When we talk about "thinking outside the box" or "expanding our minds," we mean that the brain is more than just a repository of existing knowledge; it is also a fertile field for developing unique solutions and groundbreaking insights. This metaphorical feature of the brain emphasises its ability to be creative, to break free from conventional thinking, and to explore unknown ground.

4. The Brain as a Problem-Solving Centre

Another aspect of the metaphorical representation of the brain is its function as the ultimate problem solution. It symbolises the ethos of confronting issues intellectually. When faced with difficult decisions or complex riddles, we frequently state that we must "put on our thinking caps" and activate the brain in order to find solutions.

In this metaphorical sense, the brain is analogous to a master strategist, charting a course of action through thorough study and planning. It works its way through a problem's maze, looking for patterns, determining cause and effect, and finding solutions to overcome hurdles. The metaphorical "lightbulb moment" represents the time when the brain comes up with a breakthrough solution, shedding light on previously unresolved difficulties.

5. The Brain as the Centre of Intellectual Activities

The brain is revered metaphorically as the epicentre of intellectual endeavours. It denotes the realm of mind, philosophy, and deep reflection. It is here that we wrestle with existential issues, seek insight of the human predicament, and push the boundaries of knowledge.

In this setting, the brain serves as a haven for intellectual activities. It is the intersection of philosophy, science, and art, resulting in a complex tapestry of human culture. The figurative "halls of thought" ring with intellectual debate and introspection. When people say they "engage their brains," they are implying a commitment to intellectual research and a search for greater significance.

6. The Brain as a Well of Complex Reasoning

The brain, metaphorically speaking, enters the world of advanced reasoning and cognitive powers. It is frequently described as the source of complex thought processes and advanced problem-solving skills. When we say someone has a "sharp mind" or a "brilliant brain," we are referring to their ability to think critically and intellectually.

The brain is viewed as the source of advanced reasoning and strategic thought in this metaphorical interpretation. It is where people thrive at complicated tasks like critical thinking, quantitative problem solving, and abstract reasoning. The metaphorical "wellspring of reason" refers to the brain's ability to draw on a vast reservoir of intellectual resources to address difficult and sophisticated problems.

7. The Brain as the Fulcrum of Innovation

The brain is frequently represented as the pivot of innovation and the driving force behind progress. It represents the essence of ingenuity and the ability to push forward-thinking transformation metaphorically. When we talk about "brainpower" or "brainstorming," we're talking about the communal creative energy that can result in new solutions and game-changing ideas.

The metaphorical brain is a creative powerhouse capable of igniting revolutions in technology, science, and society. It represents the source of creative energy that drives society advancement and evolution. When people "put their brains together," they are implying a joint effort to produce fresh and innovative ideas.

In short, the metaphorical portrayal of the brain demonstrates the complexity of human mind and intellectual capacity. It represents the citadel of reason, the reservoir of knowledge and creativity, the focal point of intellectual endeavours, and the well of complicated reasoning. These analogies demonstrate the breadth and complexity of human intellect, emphasising the brain's critical role in developing our awareness of the world as well as our ability to innovate and progress.

Heart

The "heart" serves as a powerful and evocative metaphor for a wide range of emotions, innermost feelings, character, and key components of the human experience. It embodies courage, resilience, and moral principles, as well as deep overtones of love, compassion, and genuineness.

1. The Heart as the Emotional Centre

Metaphorically, the heart is generally seen as the epicentre of human emotions. It is the source of our most fundamental feelings and connections, embodying love, affection, joy, and sadness. When we describe someone has a "warm heart" or a "heart of gold," we are referring to their ability to be kind, empathic, and emotionally deep. This metaphorical use emphasises the idea that our most sincere and honest emotions live in the heart.

As an emotional emblem, the heart helps us to express the depth and intensity of our sentiments. "My heart aches" refers to emotional sorrow, but "heartwarming" stories or experiences elicit feelings of joy, warmth, and profound connection.

2. The Heart as a Symbol of Love and Compassion

The heart's metaphorical position as a symbol of love and compassion is one of its most prominent. When we say we're "following our heart" or "wearing our heart on our sleeve," we're referring to the heart's function in guiding our actions and decisions based on love and empathy. In this perspective, the heart signifies the capacity for deep, selfless affection as well as the ability to connect with and care for others.

The heart also represents romantic love, with phrases like "you have my heart" or "my heart belongs to you" expressing the idea of entirely dedicating oneself to a romantic partner. The heart is widely used as a metaphorical emblem of romantic attachment in love stories and poetry.

3. The Heart as a Source of Courage and Resilience

The heart is often associated with courage, resolve, and resilience in metaphorical language. Phrases like "take heart" or "heart of a lion" conjure up images of a steadfast spirit in the face of adversity. As a symbol of strength, the heart motivates us to face problems with courage and to endure in difficult times.

When someone "puts their heart into something," it implies that they are completely committed and passionate about their efforts, emphasising the role of the heart in motivating and driving us to attain our goals.

4. The Heart as a Moral Compass

The heart functions metaphorically as a moral compass, expressing our internal sense of good and wrong. Phrases such as "have a change of heart" or "listen to your heart" imply that ethical and moral decisions are formed by matching one's inner ideals and principles. The heart represents our conscience and the decisions we make in pursuit of what we consider to be right and just.

Metaphorically, the heart drives us to act with integrity and make decisions that reflect our innermost principles. It serves as a reminder to be loyal to ourselves and to uphold our ethical ideals.

5. The Heart as an Emblem of Authenticity

In metaphorical language, the heart is also a symbol of authenticity and honesty. When we say that someone has a "heartfelt" expression or is "speaking from the heart," we mean that their feelings or words are real and unfiltered. This metaphorical application emphasises the notion that the heart is the wellspring of our most true and unpolished selves.

In this way, authenticity is inextricably linked to vulnerability and openness. When we are advised to "open our hearts," we are implying that we must allow ourselves to be emotionally available and share our actual feelings.

6. The Heart as a Source of Passion and Creativity

In metaphorical expressions, the heart is frequently associated with passion and creativity. Expressions like "pour your heart into it" imply that excitement, dedication, and emotional engagement are required for creative and artistic endeavours. The heart represents the source of inspiration and the depth of emotion that drives the creative process.

Artists, writers, singers, and innovators commonly turn to the metaphorical heart for inspiration and artistic expression. The heart symbolises the enthusiasm that drives the creative spirit.

7. The Heart as a Uniting Symbol

The heart can function as a uniting symbol in a broader context, representing the shared human experience. When we talk about "having a heart," we are referring to a shared humanity and empathy for others. The heart symbolises our interconnectedness and the value of understanding and supporting one another.

In short, the metaphorical use of the heart in human discourse spans a vast range of emotions, personality traits, and ideals. It represents love, compassion, honesty, bravery, moral ideals, honesty, passion, creativity, and the shared human experience. As a metaphorical emblem, the heart urges us to embrace our emotional depth, connect deeply with others, and make decisions that reflect our genuine selves. It honours the variety and complexities of the human experience, from the depths of our emotions to the pinnacles of our ambitions.

Mind

The "mind" is an intriguing and sophisticated metaphor that incorporates a wide range of abstract concepts, from intellect and creativity to consciousness and introspection. In human conversation, the metaphorical use of the mind enables us to go into the depths of cognition, self-awareness, and the complexities of our inner worlds.

1. The Mind as the Centre of Intellect and Thought

The mind is frequently portrayed metaphorically as the centre of intellect and thought. It represents the area of logic, logic, and cognitive processes. When we talk about someone having a "sharp mind" or making decisions "with a clear mind," we're referring to their ability to think critically, analyse, and rationally. This metaphorical use emphasises the notion that the mind is the source of intellectual exploration, where ideas are produced, conceptions are examined, and knowledge is generated.

The metaphorical representation of the mind as a warehouse of knowledge and wisdom is likewise well-developed. When we say that someone is "feeding their mind" with information or "expanding their mind," we are referring to the ongoing process of self-improvement and learning. In this way, the mind is a living reservoir of experiences, memories, and acquired wisdom.

2. The Mind as a Source of Creative Ideas

The mind is commonly associated with creativity and invention metaphorically. When we say someone has a "brilliant mind" or "a fertile mind," we are referring to their ability to develop unique and imaginative thoughts. This metaphor emphasises the mind's role as the source of creative thoughts and imaginative manifestations. It implies that the mind is more than just a place for analytical thinking; it is also a source of artistic inspiration and problem-solving resourcefulness.

3. The Mind as a Centre of Self-Awareness and Reflection

Using the mind metaphorically emphasises the mind's role as a centre of self-awareness and reflection. When someone is said to have a "deep mind" or to be "mindful," it refers to their ability to engage in introspection, self-analysis, and heightened awareness of their thoughts and feelings. This metaphor emphasises the idea that the mind is more than just a source of external information; it is also a location where we may explore our inner landscapes, examine our beliefs, and seek deeper self-understanding.

4. The Mind as a Conductor of the Inner Symphony

The mind might be viewed metaphorically as a conductor of the inner symphony of thoughts and emotions. When we say that someone's mind is "chaotic" or "well-orchestrated," we're using a metaphor to depict the organisation and harmony (or lack thereof) within their cognitive and emotional processes. In this sense, the mind serves as the conductor's baton, influencing the complicated interplay of thoughts and sensations.

5. The Mind as a Source of Inner Strength

The mind can be associated with inner strength and perseverance in metaphorical ways. When someone is considered to have a "strong mind" or "great mental discipline," it refers to their capacity to persevere in the face of hardship, keep focus, and handle it with grace. This metaphor emphasises the role of the intellect in emotional intelligence, mental fortitude, and the ability to endure life's challenges.

6. The Mind as a Source of Personal Identity

The mind can symbolise personal identity and authenticity metaphorically. When we refer to someone as "true to their mind" or "having a change of mind," we are referring to the idea that the mind is the source of one's beliefs, values, and convictions. This metaphor emphasises the necessity of matching one's thoughts and actions with one's inner ideals and the function of the mind in defining one's identity.

7. The Mind as the Nexus of Dualities

The mind can serve as a metaphor for the union of reason and emotion, logic and intuition, and analysis and empathy. When we speak of a "strong mind with a compassionate heart," we are referring to the delicate balancing of these opposing aspects within the mind. This metaphor emphasises the idea that the mind is a dynamic area where various parts of human intellect and emotion coexist and interact, rather than a rigid, one-dimensional entity.

In short, In conclusion, the metaphorical use of the mind in human discourse indicates a diverse range of abstract concepts such as intellect, creativity, self-awareness, inner strength, personal identity, and the synthesis of dualities. It invites us to delve into the depths of cognition, emotion, and awareness, emphasising the mind's important role in generating our intellectual and emotional experiences. This rich and comprehensive metaphor serves as a compelling reminder of the human psyche's complexities and diversity, encapsulating the core of our intellectual and emotional life in a single, evocative symbol.

To put it briefly, these metaphorical applications of the terms "brain," "heart," and "mind" help to express the idea that human decision-making and behaviours are impacted by a complex interaction of logic, emotions, and personal values. When making decisions, people frequently battle with balancing various factors, and these metaphors depict that inner conflict and complexity of human nature.

To gain a better understanding, consider the similarities and differences between each of these.

The triad of "brain," "heart," and "mind" metaphorically serves as a sophisticated and nuanced framework for understanding the varied facets of the human experience. Each of these metaphors is similar in that they all represent important aspects of our inner lives, decision-making, and character. They do, however, have different characteristics and are frequently employed in various circumstances to highlight specific facets of our humanity.

Similarities:

1. Symbolism of Human Experience: All three metaphors are powerful symbols that symbolise distinct aspects of the human experience. They capture the essence of our inner ideas, feelings, and complexities.

2. Inner Guidance: These metaphors are frequently used to emphasise that these inner qualities are crucial in guiding our judgements, behaviours, and moral compass. Whether it's the brain's rationality, the heart's compassion, or the mind's knowledge, they all indicate an internal source of guidance.

3. Decision-Making: Each of these metaphors is related with the decision-making process. They represent the internal strategies we employ to navigate life's difficulties.

We have the option of making decisions based on brain reasoning, heart feelings, or a synthesis of both in the mind.

4. Psychological Depth: All three metaphors encourage us to go into the psychological depths of human experience. They mirror the complexities of our inner world, which includes ideas, emotions, values, and beliefs.

Differences:

1. Emphasis on Emotion vs. Intellect:

• Heart: The heart metaphor emphasises emotions, love, compassion, and moral principles. It represents strong emotional bonds, affection, and the compassionate side of human nature.

• Brain: The metaphorical brain represents intellectual reasoning, logic, and analytical thinking. It represents the cognitive processes underlying problem solving, data processing, and objective analysis.

• Mind: In metaphorical usage, the mind signifies a blend of emotion and intelligence. It represents the interaction of cognitive and emotional aspects of human experience, emphasising a balanced and integrated approach to decision-making and comprehension.

2. Innovative Thinking and Creativity:

• Mind: The mind metaphor is frequently used to describe innovative thinking and creativity. It represents the source of fresh ideas, artistic expression, and novel solutions. It is a blend of intellectual and emotional qualities that fosters a creative and inventive attitude to life.

• Brain: While the brain is associated with logical reasoning, it may not place as much emphasis on creativity as the mind. It focuses more on problem solving and analytical thinking.

• Heart: The heart metaphor is associated with emotional depth and compassion rather than innovative thinking and creativity.

3. Balance and Synthesis:

• Mind: The mind metaphor portrays the concept of balance and synthesis in a unique way. It frequently connotes the harmonious synthesis of emotional and intellectual qualities. It implies that good decision-making and comprehension result from the interaction of reason and emotion.

• Brain and Heart: The brain and heart metaphors, on the other hand, can reflect a more dichotomous approach, in which judgements may be motivated primarily by reasoning (brain) or emotion (heart).

4. Memory and Knowledge:

• Brain: The brain can be related with memory and knowledge metaphorically. It is a storehouse of knowledge, experiences, and intellectual wisdom. It represents the cognitive part of knowledge retention, organisation, and retrieval.

• Heart and Mind: While memory and knowledge are involved, the heart and mind are more concerned with emotional and cognitive components of human experience. The heart represents emotional memory as well as the lasting influence of human bonds. Cognitive and emotional intelligence are represented by the mind.

5. Strength and Resilience:

• Heart: The heart metaphor is frequently used to depict attributes such as compassion, empathy, and moral strength. It emphasises the emotional qualities of strength, as well as the ability to empathise and connect deeply with people.

• Brain: The metaphor of the brain can refer to intellectual strength, analytical ability, and problem-solving talents. It depicts the concept of mental fortitude in the face of challenging challenges.

• Mind: In a metaphorical sense, the mind represents both intellectual and emotional resilience. It denotes the ability to navigate obstacles using a combination of cognitive and emotional power.

6. Spiritual and Philosophical Aspects:

• Mind: The mind metaphor frequently touches on philosophical and spiritual dimensions, reflecting a quest for wisdom, personal progress, and enlightenment. It represents a continuing investigation of the human condition and the goal of self-awareness.

• Brain and Heart: Although the brain and heart have philosophical and spiritual components, they are more closely related with daily decision-making and emotional

Aspect	Brain	Heart	Mind
Emotional Significance	Represents intellect, logic, and analytical thinking.	Represents emotions, compassion, and moral values.	Represents a synthesis of both emotions and intellect.
Inner Guidance	Suggests rational	Suggests emotional	Suggests a harmonious

	decision-making and analytical judgment.	depth, love, and empathy in decision-making.	balance between emotion and reason.
Decision-Making	Often implies logical and analytical decision-making.	Often implies decisions driven by deep emotions and moral values.	Implies decisions that consider both rationality and empathy.
Creativity and Innovation	May not emphasize creativity to the same extent.	Typically does not naturally lend itself to discussions of creativity or innovation.	Frequently associated with creativity and innovative thinking.
Balance and Synthesis	Often seen as a more dichotomous approach to decision-making, emphasizing rationality.	Similarly dichotomous, focusing on emotions and compassion.	Represents the harmonious integration of both emotion and reason.
Memory and Knowledge	Commonly associated with memory and knowledge.	May involve memory and knowledge but places a stronger emphasis on emotions.	Less commonly associated with memory and knowledge, emphasizing cognitive and emotional aspects.
Strength and Resilience	May relate more to intellectual strength and analytical prowess.	Often emphasizes qualities such as compassion, empathy, and moral strength.	Suggests both intellectual and emotional resilience.
Wisdom and	Not inherently	While it can be	Often linked to

Self-Discovery	associated with wisdom and self-discovery.	associated with wisdom, it does not emphasize self-discovery to the same extent.	wisdom and self-discovery, representing personal growth and enlightenment.

In conclusion,

The metaphorical use of the terms "brain," "heart," and "mind" in human language reflects the depth and diversity of human experience. While these metaphors share certain elements, they also have different emphasises. The heart symbolises feelings and compassion, the brain symbolises logic and analytical thinking, and the mind symbolises a harmonious synthesis of emotion and intellect. Each of these metaphors challenges us to investigate different aspects of our inner worlds, providing a more complex view of how we navigate life, make decisions, and connect with others.

Dreams, Goals and Achievements

Dreams, goals, and achievements are all interwoven notions that shape our lives and provide us with a feeling of purpose and direction. Here's an explanation of these terms:

1. Dreams:

• Dreams are our ambitions, aspirations, and visions of what we hope to accomplish or experience in the future.

• Dreams can cover a wide range of topics, including personal, professional, and even spiritual fulfilment.

• Dreams frequently mirror our deepest wishes and can provide motivation and inspiration.

2. Goals:

• Goals are definite, quantifiable, and time-bound targets that are set to assist us in realising our dreams.

• They provide a clear blueprint and direction for our actions, guiding us towards the outcomes we desire.

• Goals can be short-term or long-term in nature, and they assist us in breaking down our aspirations into doable steps.

3. Achievements:

• Achievements are the outputs or outcomes of our efforts and activities as we move towards our objectives and dreams.

• Fulfilment, contentment, and achievement can result from achieving a goal or desire.

• Achievements can be personal, professional, educational, or in any other field.

Let us go over each of these in greater detail.

The word "dreams" refers to a person's future aspirations, long-term goals, and wishes. These are the things that people wish to do or experience in their lives, and they represent their ideal visions or desires. Dreams frequently include the following:

1. Aspirations: Dreams are the lofty goals and aspirations that people have for themselves. Individuals may endeavour to achieve job goals, personal successes, and life milestones.

2. Objectives: Dreams frequently represent a person's objectives and goals for their lives. These goals can range from professional achievement to making a positive difference in the world.

3. Long-Term Goals: Dreams are often long-term goals that people work towards throughout time. They provide a sense of purpose and direction, directing one's behaviours and decisions.

4. Personal Fulfilment: Personal fulfilment and happiness may be included in dreams. People may wish to discover love, happiness, and to live a meaningful and content life.

5. Ideal Visions: Dreams frequently reveal a person's ideal future vision. These ambitions may include not only financial achievement, but also personal development, self-discovery, and the pursuit of a meaningful and rewarding life.

6. Hopes and Wishes: Dreams are the deepest hopes and wishes that people have for themselves and others they love. Aspirations can be both individual and social.

Thus, "dreams" are a mirror of one's deepest aspirations and driving forces. They serve as a source of inspiration, motivating people to strive for a brighter future and make their ideal ideas a reality. Dreams can differ greatly from person to person and can be impacted by cultural, societal, and personal variables, making them intensely personal and unique to each person.

Beyond the actual completion of chores or sporting events, the term "goals" refers to specific objectives, targets, or milestones that individuals set for themselves in numerous parts of life. Goals can be defined as:

1. Life Objectives: Goals are similar to life aims or broad purposes. They signify what people desire to achieve or the path they want their life to pursue. Someone's goal, for example, could be to live a happy, fulfilled life.

2. Personal Development: Goals can represent the concept of personal development and self-improvement. They could represent the road of becoming a better person, learning new talents, or gaining knowledge.

3. Career and Ambitions: Metaphorical aims are frequently associated with career aspirations and ambitions. They represent the professional milestones and achievements that one desires, such as obtaining a specific position, launching a firm, or having a big contribution in a particular subject.

4. Relationships: Goals can also apply to personal relationships. They represent the desired goals or milestones in one's interactions with others, such as making meaningful connections, strengthening communication, or developing strong, lasting relationships, in this context.

5. Health and Well-being: Goals can refer to health and well-being objectives in a metaphorical sense. This covers physical fitness, mental health, and general wellness, with objectives such as living a healthy lifestyle or finding balance.

6. Personal Satisfaction: Achieving goals represents personal fulfilment and satisfaction. These objectives indicate what gives one's life significance and contentment.

7. Success Vision: Goals conceptually embody one's success vision and the steps required to achieve it. They operate as guides for making choices, decisions, and actions that are in line with the vision.

8. Contribution and Impact: For some people, goals express their desire to have a good impact on society or the world, emphasising the larger purpose of their actions and achievements.

Thus, goals are not restricted to precise, measurable targets, but are broader and incorporate the essence of what individuals desire to achieve, experience, or become in their lives. They provide purpose, direction, and inspiration in various facets of life.

The term "achievements" has a larger, more abstract meaning than its precise sense of physical, measurable triumphs. Achievements can refer to a variety of personal, professional, or symbolic successes that have meaning in a person's life or in a specific environment. Here are several definitions of achievements:

1. **Personal Development:** Achievements can serve as stepping stones in one's personal development. Overcoming obstacles, learning new skills, or deepening one's understanding of oneself can all be regarded metaphorical achievements.

2. **Learning and Knowledge:** Acquiring knowledge, developing insights, and reaching intellectual milestones can all be viewed as metaphorical achievements. This could include a greater grasp of the world, personal philosophy, or a specific topic.

3. **Emotional and Spiritual Fulfilment:** Achievements can also represent inner peace, satisfaction, or a sense of fulfilment in the emotional and spiritual realms. Achieving a state of happiness, balance, or harmony may be regarded as a metaphorical achievement.

4. **Relationships and Connections:** Building meaningful relationships, fostering connections with people, and maintaining healthy interactions can all be considered as metaphorical achievements. These achievements go beyond the concrete and highlight the emotional and social aspects of one's life.

5. **Legacy and Impact:** Leaving a beneficial impression on others, contributing to the well-being of a community, or leaving a lasting legacy can all be considered metaphorical achievements. These achievements demonstrate the broader impact and significance of one's efforts.

6. **Defying Adversity:** Successfully navigating and conquering challenges, setbacks, or adversity can be viewed as a metaphorical achievement. It exemplifies resilience,

strength, and the ability to persevere in the face of adversity.

7. Artistic and Creative Expression: Achievements for artists and creatives may include expressing oneself through various types of art. Creating something significant, inspiring emotions, or pushing the limits of creativity can all be considered metaphorical achievements.

8. Philanthropy and Volunteerism: Acts of compassion, contributions to the wellbeing of others, and participation in humanitarian endeavours can all be regarded metaphorical achievements. These behaviours demonstrate a commitment to making a positive difference in the world.

9. Balance and Well-Being: Achieving a feeling of balance in life, controlling stress, and preserving overall well-being can all be metaphorical achievements. This demonstrates a comprehensive approach to personal fulfilment and happiness.

10. Adaptability and Innovation: Embracing change, adapting to new circumstances, and fostering creativity can all be metaphorical achievements. These achievements demonstrate the ability to negotiate complexity and survive in changing situations.

In essence, achievements go beyond simply external markers of success and dive into the subjective, intimate, and profoundly meaningful parts of a person's life experience. They include a diverse range of experiences and achievements that contribute to personal fulfilment, progress, and the general richness of one's life.

Dreams, goals, and achievements constitute a dynamic cycle that moulds and motivates our life, in a metaphorical sense. This interdependence can be explained as follows:

1. Dreams:

•Dreams represent an individual's broad vision of what they want to achieve or the life they want to live. These dreams include their deepest wants, long-term goals, and idealised futures.

•Dreams serve as the cycle's starting point, offering the initial inspiration and motivation. They provide people a sense of purpose and direction, pointing them in the direction of something worthwhile and gratifying.

2. Goals:

• Goals are the actual, actionable measures that people take to make their goals a reality. Goals stem from and are linked with one's dreams. They break down the big picture into smaller, more attainable, measurable, and time-bound objectives.

• Goals provide individuals with a path and direction as they work towards their dreams. They act as a link between aspirations and concrete progress, assisting in the effective allocation of effort and resources.

3. Achievements:

• Achievements are the measurable results of pursuing goals. They symbolise the milestones and victories that people achieve as they work towards their dreams.

• Achievements provide a sense of fulfilment, satisfaction, and success, reinforcing the perception that people are making progress towards their dreams.

The relationship between dreams, goals and achievements can be thought of as a never-ending cycle:

• Dreams motivate people to develop goals that are in line with their vision, giving them a clear way forward.

• Goals help people focus their efforts, prioritise actions, and make steady progress towards their dreams.

• Achievements, in turn, validate and celebrate progress made, inspiring individuals to pursue their dreams or adjust their goals in light of fresh insights and experiences.

A tabular representation of the interrelationship between dreams, goals, and achievements:

Aspect	Dreams	Goals	Achievements
Definition	Aspirations, idealized future	Specific, measurable targets	Tangible outcomes
Role	Inspirational, visionary	Directional, actionable	Validating, motivating
Influence	Source of inspiration	Roadmap to realization	Feedback on progress
Significance	Provide purpose and vision	Translate vision into action	Confirm progress
Motivation	Initiates motivation	Sustains motivation	Enhances motivation
Reflection	Reflect values and beliefs	Reflect priorities	Reflect success and growth
Adaptability	May evolve over time	Can be adjusted as needed	Inform future aspirations
Resilience	Maintain motivation in	Adapt goals to overcome	Validate perseverance

	face of setbacks	obstacles	
Balancing	May encompass personal and professional aspirations	Aligns and balances pursuits in both spheres	Reflects success in both domains
Legacy & Contribution	May lead to a lasting impact	Achieving dreams beyond personal satisfaction	Impact on society and legacy
Lifetime Perspective	Evolve and mature over a lifetime	Goals set and adapted at different life stages	Journey of self-discovery
Outcome	Self-discovery, fulfillment	Progress towards the realization of dreams	Sense of accomplishment

This cycle is adaptive and dynamic. It encourages people to stay focused on their overarching dreams while also providing a methodical way to realising them. Individuals may establish new, higher goals or broaden their dreams as they achieve their goals and experience achievements, sustaining the cycle of growth, aspiration, and fulfilment.

Setting clear and attainable goals, working diligently to achieve those goals, and enjoying accomplishments along the way are common steps in making dreams a reality. When it comes to dreams, goals, and achievements, here are some crucial elements to consider:

• Clarity: Define your dreams clearly and divide them into specific, actionable targets. The more detailed and measurable your goals, the easier it will be to achieve them.

- Motivation: Your dreams can be a great source of motivation. They provide you a cause to persevere in the face of obstacles and disappointments as you strive towards your goals.
- Persistence: Achieving big objectives and goals frequently necessitates perseverance and a willingness to overcome barriers and disappointments.
- Adaptability: Be willing to adapt your aims and dreams as circumstances change. A diversion might sometimes lead to a new and equally rewarding path.
- Recognise and Celebrate Your Achievements: Recognise and celebrate your accomplishments, no matter how minor they may appear. Recognising your progress can help you stay motivated and confident.
- Maintaining a sense of balance in your life is as crucial as chasing your desires and goals. Other areas of your well-being, such as health, relationships, and personal development, should not be overlooked.

To summarise, dreams motivate us, goals guide us, and achievements are the tangible fruits of our efforts. These aspects interact to foster personal growth and fulfilment, assisting us in living a meaningful and purposeful life.

Strong Mind and Willpower

Strong mind and willpower are necessary traits that can enable people to overcome obstacles, accomplish their objectives, and live more purposeful and disciplined lives. Here's a summary of what these attributes include:

1. Strong Mind:

• **Resilience:** A strong mind is able to overcome hardship and disappointments. It entails having the capacity to adjust and maintain emotional stability in the face of difficulties.

• **Emotional Intelligence:** A crucial component of a strong mind is the ability to comprehend and regulate one's own emotions as well as those of others. Better decision-making and interpersonal interactions may result from this.

• **Mental Toughness:** Having a strong mind is often linked to having mental toughness, which enables people to face challenges head-on and resist giving in to negative thoughts or self-doubt.

2. Willpower:

• **Self-Discipline:** Willpower and self-discipline go hand in hand. It's the capacity to restrain one's desires and maintain concentration on long-term objectives in the face of transient temptations.

• **Delayed Gratification:** People with willpower are able to postpone receiving rewards right away in favour of bigger, more significant rewards down the road. In order to succeed over the long run, this is essential.

- **Making Better Decisions:** Willpower aids in decision-making by preventing rash decisions and taking actions' effects into account.

The following are some methods for boosting your Mind and Willpower:

- **Establish Specific Goals:** Clearly state your goals and lay out a plan for reaching them. This may give you inspiration and guidance.

- **Exercise Self-Control:** Teach yourself to put off short-term pleasure in favour of long-term gains. Exercises like mindfulness, meditation, and imposing boundaries on impulsive actions might help achieve this.

- **Create Healthy routines:** Creating wholesome routines can help you use less willpower all the time. Maintaining self-discipline can be facilitated by routine and planning.

- **Seek Support:** Encircle yourself with mentors, family members, or friends who can hold you accountable and offer encouragement.

- **Remain Positive:** Your willpower can be greatly impacted by having a positive outlook and strong self-belief. Develop optimism and self-assurance in your capacity to overcome obstacles.

- **Take Lessons from Failures:** Every journey involves failures and setbacks. Rather than giving up, see them as chances to develop and learn, and then apply what you've learned to your strategy.

- **Remain Mindful:** Making deliberate decisions and practising self-control can be aided by being conscious of your thoughts, feelings, and impulses.

Keep in mind that developing a strong mind and willpower is a continuous process. Though it requires patience, practise, and commitment, it can result in increased self-control, personal development, and the capacity to realise your goals.

The significance of Strong Mind and Willpower:

A strong mind and willpower are important qualities that can help people overcome obstacles, achieve their goals, and live more fulfilling lives. Here are some important characteristics of a strong mind and willpower:

1. **Self-discipline:** Willpower is inextricably linked with self-discipline. It entails being able to control your impulses, stay focused on long-term goals, and resist temptations or distractions that may impede your progress.

2. **Determination:** A strong mind is focused and determined. It is the attitude that says, "I will not give up, no matter how difficult the journey may be." Determination allows you to persevere in the face of setbacks and failures.

3. **Goal-setting:** It is critical to have a clear sense of purpose and well-defined goals in order to channel your willpower in a productive direction. Goals that are SMART (Specific, Measurable, Achievable, Relevant, and Time-bound) can help you stay motivated and focused.

4. **Mental resilience:** A strong mind is resilient and capable of overcoming adversity. It is about approaching obstacles with a positive attitude, learning from mistakes, and adapting to changing circumstances.

5. **Positive mindset:** Developing a positive and optimistic outlook can help to boost your willpower. A positive

mindset can help you stay motivated and believe that you can overcome challenges.

6. Stress management: Stress management and finding healthy ways to deal with life's pressures are critical for maintaining strong willpower. Stress can sap your mental energy, making it difficult to stay on track.

7. Self-awareness: Recognising your triggers for impulsivity or procrastination, as well as understanding your strengths and weaknesses, is critical for improving your willpower. Self-awareness allows you to make proactive decisions.

8. Mindfulness and meditation: Mindfulness and meditation are practises that can help train your mind to focus, reduce distractions, and improve your ability to stay committed to your goals.

9. Resisting instant gratification: One of the ultimate tests of willpower is the ability to forego immediate gratification in favour of long-term gains. This necessitates the discipline of making sacrifices now for a brighter future.

10. Support systems: Surround yourself with a supportive network of friends, family, or mentors to provide encouragement and accountability, allowing you to stay on track.

Developing a strong mind and willpower is a never-ending process that requires self-improvement, self-reflection, and consistent effort. It's a valuable set of skills that can lead to personal development, accomplishment, and a greater sense of control over your life.

Now, let us go over strong mind and willpower in greater detail.

Strong Mind

A strong mind is a multifaceted concept that includes a variety of mental and psychological characteristics such as resilience, emotional intelligence, cognitive abilities, adaptability, and tenacity. It is a mental state of well-being and fortitude that allows a person to face challenges, overcome adversity, and maintain a positive outlook in the face of life's complexities.

A strong mind is a quality that can be developed and cultivated throughout one's life, rather than a static trait. It entails a set of mental and emotional skills that enable people to thrive in their personal lives as well as in the face of professional or societal pressures. In this piece of writing, we will look at the components of a strong mind, their significance, and provide examples to demonstrate these ideas.

Characteristics of a Strong Mind:

1. Resilience: A strong mind must have resilience. It refers to a person's ability to recover from setbacks, adversity, and stressful situations. Failures do not define resilient people; instead, they serve as opportunities for growth. When faced with a challenge, they maintain their cool and emotional equilibrium.

Example: A student who experiences academic setbacks but perseveres and maintains a positive attitude, eventually achieving success.

2. Emotional Intelligence: The ability to recognise, understand, manage, and navigate one's own emotions as well as the emotions of others is referred to as emotional intelligence. People who have a strong mind can maintain healthy relationships, empathise with others, and manage their own emotional responses effectively.

Example: A manager who can de-escalate team conflicts by understanding and addressing team members' emotional needs.

3. Determination and Willpower: A strong mind requires determination and willpower. Setting clear goals, staying focused, and having the tenacity to pursue those goals in the face of obstacles and temptations are all part of it.

Example: An athlete who trains tirelessly and follows a strict diet in order to compete in the Olympics.

4. Positive Mindset: A positive mindset is defined by optimism, the ability to see opportunities in challenges, and a general sense of hope and confidence in one's abilities.

Example: A cancer patient who maintains a positive attitude throughout treatment and believes in his or her ability to recover.

5. Adaptability: A strong mind is adaptable, meaning it can deal with change and uncertainty. This entails being able to change one's mindset, strategies, and actions in response to changing circumstances.

Example: An entrepreneur who changes their business model in response to market trends and technological advancements.

6. Self-Control and Discipline: Self-control and discipline are necessary for resisting temptations, delaying gratification, and making long-term decisions that may not yield immediate benefits.

Example: A person who diligently saves money in order to achieve a long-term financial goal, such as purchasing a home.

7. Stress Management: Maintaining a strong mind requires effective stress management. It incorporates coping mechanisms, relaxation techniques, and mindfulness practises to reduce stress and prevent its negative effects on mental health.

Example: A busy executive who meditates and practises yoga on a daily basis to cope with the stress of a high-pressure job.

8. Self-Awareness: The ability to understand one's own strengths, weaknesses, triggers, and areas for improvement is referred to as self-awareness. It serves as the foundation for personal development and self-improvement.

Example: A person who recognises and actively works on strategies to control their impulsive behaviour.

The Value of a Strong Mind:

A strong mind is extremely valuable in many aspects of life. Here are a few examples of why having a strong mind is highly valued:

1. Adversity Resilience: Life is full of challenges, setbacks, and unexpected obstacles. A strong mind enables people to face challenges with courage and determination, ultimately leading to personal growth and success.

Example: Nelson Mandela, who spent 27 years in prison before emerging with a strong mind and leading South Africa through a peaceful transition to democracy.

2. Mental Health and Well-Being: Having a strong mind is closely related to having good mental health and well-being. It can help people manage stress, anxiety, and depression while also maintaining a positive outlook on life.

Example: People who have been through traumatic experiences and sought therapy in order to develop a strong mind and regain their mental health.

3. Personal and Professional Success: People with strong minds are more likely to be successful in their personal and professional lives. They are more adept at setting and achieving goals, maintaining healthy relationships, and navigating the modern world's complexities.

Example: Elon Musk is well-known for his tenacity and perseverance in founding and leading several successful companies, including SpaceX and Tesla.

4. Leadership: Strong-minded people are often effective leaders. Their strong mind is demonstrated by their ability to remain calm under pressure, make sound decisions, and inspire others.

Example: Mahatma Gandhi, who led India to independence through nonviolent resistance, exemplified extraordinary resilience and determination in his leadership.

5. Dealing with Change: In a world of rapid change and uncertainty, a strong mind enables people to adapt, innovate, and thrive in changing circumstances.

Example: Steve Jobs, the man who, with the launch of the iPhone, revolutionised the technology industry through his adaptability and vision.

Examples of a Strong Mind in Action:

1. Malala Yousafzai: In the face of adversity, Malala, a Pakistani activist for female education, demonstrated incredible determination and resilience. She survived a Taliban assassination attempt and continued to advocate for girls' education. Her strong mind propelled her to the position of youngest-ever Nobel Prize laureate.

2. Winston Churchill: During World War II, as Prime Minister of the United Kingdom, Churchill demonstrated unwavering determination, resilience, and a positive mindset in the face of great global turmoil. His strong mind inspired his country to fight on and eventually win the war.

3. Stephen Hawking: Despite suffering from a debilitating motor neuron disease, renowned theoretical physicist Stephen Hawking maintained a positive attitude and continued his groundbreaking work on cosmology and black holes. His strong mind enabled him to overcome physical constraints.

4. J.K. Rowling: Before becoming famous as the author of the Harry Potter series, J.K. Rowling was rejected by numerous publishers. Her perseverance, adaptability, and self-belief helped her become one of history's best-selling authors.

5. Nelson Mandela: Mandela was imprisoned for 27 years for his anti-apartheid activities. During his confinement, he developed the fortitude and determination that would eventually lead to his successful fight against apartheid and election as South Africa's first black president.

6. Angela Merkel: As Chancellor of Germany, Angela Merkel was known for her methodical as well as calm leadership style. Her sharp mind enabled her to navigate complicated political situations and guide Germany through difficult times.

7. Michael Jordan: Widely regarded as one of the greatest basketball players of all time, Michael Jordan's unwavering work ethic, discipline, and determination on and off the court demonstrate the value of a strong mind in achieving success.

8. Anne Frank: Through her writings, Anne Frank, a Jewish girl who documented her experiences in hiding during the Holocaust, demonstrated tremendous character strength. Her ability to maintain hope and optimism in the face of adversity demonstrates a strong mind.

These real-world examples demonstrate how a strong mind can manifest itself.

Willpower

Willpower, also known as self-control or self-discipline, is an important aspect of human psychology that influences personal and professional success, goal achievement, and overall well-being. It entails being able to control one's impulses, make deliberate choices, and resist instant gratification in pursuit of long-term goals.

Willpower is the mental muscle that enables people to overcome obstacles, manage temptations, and stay focused on their goals. In this piece of writing, we will look at its psychological underpinnings, factors that influence it, the science behind it, and practical strategies for strengthening and harnessing this important aspect of human behaviour. We will demonstrate the importance of willpower and how it can be used to overcome obstacles and achieve personal and professional goals using a variety of real-life examples.

The Elements of Willpower

Willpower is a multifaceted concept that includes the following elements:

1. **Inhibitory Control:** This characteristic of willpower refers to the ability to inhibit or suppress impulsive or unwanted thoughts, emotions, or actions. It enables people to resist immediate temptations that may jeopardise their long-term goals.

2. **Initiative Control:** The ability to initiate and sustain action towards a specific goal is referred to as initiative control. It entails the motivation to begin and continue with tasks that may not yield immediate rewards.

3. **Attention Control:** Willpower also includes the ability to focus and direct one's attention away from distractions and towards relevant tasks. Maintaining concentration on the desired goal requires attention control.

4. **Emotion Regulation:** The ability to manage and modulate one's emotional responses is referred to as emotion regulation. It entails dealing with stress, frustration, and other negative emotions in a way that doesn't compromise goal achievement.

5. Decision-Making: One of the most important aspects of willpower is the ability to make deliberate, rational decisions that align with one's long-term goals.

The Psychology of Willpower

Understanding the psychological underpinnings of willpower is critical for harnessing and strengthening this capacity.

1. Theory of Ego Depletion

The Ego Depletion Theory, proposed by Roy F. Baumeister, is one of the most well-known theories related to willpower. According to this theory, self-control and willpower are finite resources that can be depleted with use. In other words, making a lot of decisions or exercising self-control in one area of life can lead to less self-control in other areas.

For example, if a person spends their day resisting the temptation to eat unhealthy snacks, it may be more difficult for them to muster the willpower to complete a demanding work task later in the day. This depletion effect is thought to occur because different types of self-control use the same pool of self-regulatory resources.

2. The Strength Model of Willpower

According to the Strength Model of Willpower, proposed by Baumeister and John Tierney in their book "Willpower: Rediscovering the Greatest Human Strength," willpower is like a muscle that can be strengthened through training and practise. This model contends that, similar to physical muscles, willpower can be depleted but also developed and improved over time.

The more a person uses their willpower, the stronger it becomes. Engaging in self-control tasks, such as developing good habits or making healthy choices, can improve one's overall capacity for willpower. This model takes a more optimistic approach, emphasising that willpower is a trait that can be developed and expanded rather than a limited resource.

The Science of Willpower

1. Brain Regions and the Concept of Willpower

Specific brain regions associated with willpower have been identified through neuroimaging studies. The prefrontal cortex, particularly the dorsolateral prefrontal cortex, is important for executive functions such as decision-making, inhibitory control, and attention. This part of the brain is responsible for self-regulation and resisting temptations.

Furthermore, the ventromedial prefrontal cortex is associated with evaluating the value and rewards associated with various choices. The interaction of these brain regions affects an individual's ability to exercise self-control and make decisions that are in line with their long-term goals.

2. Neurotransmitters and the Concept of Willpower

Neurotransmitters such as dopamine and serotonin also have an impact on willpower. Dopamine, which is associated with reward and motivation, helps to reinforce positive behaviours and goal attainment. Serotonin, which affects mood and emotional stability, can have an impact on an individual's emotional regulation and, as a result, their ability to self-control.

3. Glucose and the Concept of Willpower

The availability of glucose, the brain's primary energy source, has been linked to willpower. According to research, tasks that require self-control can deplete glucose levels, potentially contributing to ego depletion. Consuming glucose or other energy sources can help replenish self-control resources, providing a temporary boost in willpower.

Influencing Factors on Willpower

Willpower is influenced by a variety of external and internal factors.

1. Aspects of Environment

A person's willpower can be greatly impacted by their surroundings. Having to resist temptations or other distractions can make self-control harder to maintain. For instance, someone who is attempting to follow a healthy diet could struggle if they are surrounded by junk food.

A supportive and structured environment, on the other hand, can promote willpower. An individual's ability to focus and exercise self-control can be improved if their workspace is organised, free of distractions, and conducive to their work.

2. Motivation and Goal Clarity

Motivation and goal clarity are important factors in determining willpower. People's willpower is significantly increased when they have a clear sense of their goals and are deeply motivated to achieve them. Motivation is the driving force that keeps self-control efforts going even when faced with obstacles.

3. Stress and Willpower

Stress can have a negative impact on willpower. Stress can deplete self-control resources, making it more difficult to resist temptations and make disciplined decisions. Stress management and reduction techniques, such as mindfulness and relaxation techniques, can help mitigate this effect.

4. Sleep and Willpower

An individual's willpower can be harmed by a lack of sleep. Sleep deprivation has an impact on cognitive functions such as decision-making and inhibitory control. Maintaining a strong willpower requires adequate rest.

The Crucial Role of Willpower in Goal Achievement

Willpower is essential in achieving personal and professional goals. It gives people the ability to:

1. Overcome Procrastination: Procrastination is frequently caused by a lack of self-control. Willpower enables people to begin tasks quickly and persevere in their completion.

2. Create and Maintain Healthy Habits: Creating and maintaining healthy habits, such as exercising regularly or eating a balanced diet, requires self-discipline and willpower.

3. Long-Term Success: Many significant accomplishments, whether in education, career, or personal development, are the result of consistent effort and self-control over time.

4. Resist Temptations: The ability to resist temptations, whether related to unhealthy habits, impulsive spending, or distractions, demonstrates strong willpower.

5. Make Sound Financial Decisions: Prudent financial decisions require self-control and willpower, such as saving, investing, and avoiding impulsive spending.

Examples of Willpower in Action

1. Mahatma Gandhi: Throughout his life, Mahatma Gandhi, the iconic leader of India's independence movement, demonstrated remarkable willpower. Even in the face of adversity, violence, and imprisonment, his commitment to nonviolent resistance to British colonial rule was unwavering. Gandhi's ability to persevere in his pursuit of justice and independence for India demonstrates the strength of willpower in the face of formidable obstacles.

2. Angela Duckworth: Angela Duckworth, a psychologist, coined the term "grit" to describe a combination of passion and perseverance. Her research has highlighted the importance of perseverance and self-control in achieving long-term goals. Duckworth's own path from a teaching career to groundbreaking research exemplifies her personal dedication to her goals, which she attributes to exceptional willpower.

3. Michael Phelps: Michael Phelps, the most decorated Olympian in history, showed incredible determination in his pursuit of swimming excellence. His rigorous training regimen, strict dietary discipline, and unwavering commitment to his sport enabled him to win 23 Olympic gold medals. Phelps' ability to maintain peak performance across multiple Olympic Games exemplifies the power of willpower in sustaining excellence.

4. Marie Kondo: Marie Kondo is a Japanese organising consultant and author best known for her revolutionary

KonMari method of decluttering and cleaning. Her success in introducing a new approach to home organisation and assisting people in changing their lives through tidiness is a testament to her perseverance and self-discipline.

5. Warren Buffett: One of the world's most successful investors, Warren Buffett, is frequently cited for his remarkable self-control and long-term focus. Despite his enormous wealth, he leads a modest life and adheres to his investment principles. Buffett's ability to resist the allure of excessive spending and speculative investments is an excellent example of the role of willpower in financial success.

Boosting Willpower

Willpower development is a worthwhile endeavour that can lead to improved self-control and a greater ability to achieve personal and professional objectives.

1. Goal Setting: Setting clear, well-defined goals provides direction and motivation for willpower exertion. Setting SMART (Specific, Measurable, Achievable, Relevant, Time-bound) goals can boost one's commitment and self-control.

2. Creating Routines and Habits: Developing structured routines and positive habits can help to reduce the reliance on willpower for daily decision-making. Individuals save their self-control resources for more significant challenges by automating certain behaviours.

3. Mindfulness and Meditation: Mindfulness and meditation can help with self-awareness and emotional regulation, which can lead to better self-control. These techniques assist people in remaining focused and composed in the face of temptations or stress.

4. Self-Monitoring and Accountability: Tracking progress and holding oneself or others accountable can help boost willpower. Using journals, apps, or social support to track goals and commitments, for example, can help to reinforce self-discipline.

5. Self-Care and Stress Management: It is critical to prioritise self-care, which includes adequate sleep, regular exercise, and stress management techniques, in order to maintain a strong willpower. Reduced stress and overall well-being help to improve self-control.

6. Gradual Exposure: Gradual exposure to difficult situations or temptations can help people develop resilience and willpower. Over time, incremental steps allow for the development of self-control.

In conclusion, willpower is a fundamental human capacity that, when harnessed and developed, can enable individuals to overcome obstacles, make disciplined choices, and achieve their goals. It is a mental muscle that, like physical muscles, can be strengthened and trained with practise and dedication. Willpower development is a lifelong journey that can lead to personal growth, accomplishment, and a greater sense of self-control.

A strong mind and willpower are inextricably linked and frequently go hand in hand. They are both important components of a person's mental and emotional toughness, and they reinforce each other in a variety of ways. Here is how they are related:

1. Willpower as a Component of a Strong Mind: Willpower is one of the key components that contribute to overall mental strength. A strong mind is capable of exercising self-control, making disciplined decisions, and resisting immediate gratification. Willpower is the mental muscle that allows a strong mind to remain focused on long-term goals despite distractions or challenges.

2. Resilience and Determination: Both strong mind and willpower encompass resilience and determination. Resilience is the ability to recover from setbacks, and determination is the determination to persevere in the pursuit of goals. Willpower is essential in maintaining resilience and determination. It is the force that enables people to stay focused on their goals and overcome adversity.

3. Self-Control and Discipline: Willpower is frequently referred to as self-control or self-discipline. A strong mind is born with the self-control and discipline needed to make decisions that are consistent with long-term values and priorities. This includes resisting temptation, controlling impulses, and staying focused.

4. Goal Achievement: Willpower is a major motivator for goal achievement, and a strong mind is defined by the ability to set and achieve meaningful goals. Individuals with strong minds use willpower to initiate and sustain the effort required to achieve these objectives. Willpower and a strong mind work in tandem to drive success in education, career, personal development, and other life domains.

5. Emotional Regulation: A strong mind frequently includes emotional intelligence and the ability to effectively regulate one's emotions. Willpower is essential for maintaining emotional equilibrium, especially in stressful or emotionally challenging situations. It enables people to manage their reactions and make thoughtful decisions even when their emotions are high.

6. Maintaining a Positive and Optimistic Attitude: A strong mind and willpower both contribute to maintaining a positive and optimistic outlook. Even when faced with difficulties, a strong mind remains optimistic and focused on solutions. Willpower contributes to this positive mindset by resisting negative thought patterns and the temptation to succumb to pessimism.

7. Overcoming Temptation: Willpower refers to the ability to resist immediate temptations in favour of long-term goals, and it is an essential component of a strong mind. A strong mind enables people to make decisions that are in their best interests, even when faced with tempting alternatives.

8. Resisting Instant Gratification: It takes a strong mind and willpower to resist instant gratification. They enable people to put off rewards or pleasures in order to achieve more significant, long-term goals. This is an important aspect of personal development and achievement.

In conclusion,

A strong mind and willpower are intertwined qualities that complement and reinforce one another. A strong mind combines mental and emotional characteristics such as resilience, determination, emotional intelligence, and a positive outlook. Willpower, on the other hand, is the practical manifestation of these characteristics, allowing people to exercise self-control, make disciplined choices, and persevere in the face of adversity. A powerful combination of a strong mind and willpower can lead to personal growth, achievement, and a greater sense of control over one's life.

Overpopulation and Underemployment

Overpopulation and underemployment are complex and interconnected issues that have ramifications for social, economic, and environmental aspects of society. Let's look at each of these issues separately and then consider how they might interact.

Overpopulation:

Overpopulation occurs when the number of people in a given geographic area exceeds the carrying capacity of the environment, resulting in a variety of negative consequences. Carrying capacity is the maximum population size that an environment can sustainably support given available resources, technology, and social organisation at the time.

The following are some of the key characteristics and issues associated with overpopulation:

1. **Resource Scarcity:** Increased demand for essential resources such as food, water, energy, and raw materials can result from overpopulation. When demand exceeds available supply, it can lead to scarcity, competition, and potential resource depletion.

2. **Environmental Impact:** Overpopulation has a significant environmental impact. Human activities such as deforestation, pollution, and habitat destruction can all contribute to environmental degradation, biodiversity loss, and climate change.

3. Urbanisation Issues: Overpopulation frequently results in rapid urbanisation as people migrate to cities in search of better opportunities. This can put a strain on urban infrastructure, resulting in issues such as traffic congestion, insufficient housing, and insufficient public services.

4. Health Concerns: Disease transmission can be facilitated in densely populated areas due to close human contact. Access to healthcare may become difficult, resulting in public health issues.

5. Social and Economic Consequences: Overpopulation can lead to poverty, unemployment, and social unrest. Because of the strain on resources and services, there may be an unequal distribution of wealth and opportunities.

It is important to note that overpopulation is a relative concept, as technological advancements, changes in lifestyle, and the ability to manage resources sustainably can all influence an environment's carrying capacity. Furthermore, depending on factors such as governance, economic development, and social policies, different regions and countries may experience overpopulation in different ways.

Efforts to combat overpopulation frequently include family planning, education, healthcare and sustainable development strategies to ensure a balance between human population size and the capacity of the environment to support it.

Numerous factors contribute to overpopulation, and the exact causes can differ amongst nations and regions. The following are some typical causes of overpopulation:

1. High Birth Rates: High birth rates frequently play a major role in the overpopulation problem. Cultural, social, religious, and economic factors can all have an impact on this. Higher birth rates can also be caused by limited access to family planning services and education.

2. Drop in Death Rates: Medical, sanitary, and healthcare advancements have resulted in a drop in mortality rates. The population as a whole grows as more people live to adulthood and old age.

3. Lack of Education: Higher birth rates may be observed in areas with lower levels of education. Larger families may be a result of ignorance about family planning options and the advantages of having fewer children.

4. Cultural and Religious Beliefs: Attitudes regarding the size of a family can be greatly influenced by cultural and religious beliefs. Having more children may be viewed as desirable or in line with religious teachings in some cultures.

5. Economic Factors: Occasionally, economic factors may be a contributing factor to overpopulation. For instance, larger families might be considered advantageous for tending to the land in agrarian societies. Furthermore, in some developing economies, having children can be seen as an investment in social security for the future.

6. Lack of Family Planning Services: Unplanned pregnancies and larger family sizes may result from restricted access to family planning services and contraceptives. Cultural resistance, availability, and cost are some of the barriers that may affect how family planning resources are used.

7. Social and Gender Norms: Conventional gender roles and cultural norms that place a premium on procreation, especially for women, may be a factor in the increased birth rate.

8. Political and Social Instability: Areas prone to social unrest, conflict, or political instability may see delays in family planning and healthcare services, which raises the birth rate.

9. Poverty: Overpopulation can both cause and be a result of poverty. On the other hand, overpopulation can exacerbate economic hardship and poverty. Large families may be perceived as a source of financial support.

10. Migration: The dynamics of the population can be impacted by patterns of migration. Certain areas may become overpopulated due to high immigration rates, either within the same region or to urban areas.

It is essential to understand that there are many interrelated and complex factors causing overpopulation. In order to effectively combat overpopulation, a multimodal strategy that incorporates family planning services accessibility, healthcare, education, and economic development is usually needed. Encouraging people and communities to make knowledgeable decisions about the size of their families is a common component of sustainable solutions.

Overpopulation can lead to a variety of problems that affect societies, economies, and the environment. Here are some of the key problems associated with overpopulation:

1. Scarcity of Resources: An excessive number of people places a great deal of strain on vital resources like food, water, energy, and raw materials. This may cause these resources to become scarcer, more competitive, and eventually deplete.

2. **Environmental Degradation:** To accommodate a growing population, human activity has expanded and resource demand has increased, which can lead to environmental degradation. Common outcomes include deforestation, pollution, habitat destruction, and biodiversity loss.

3. **Water Shortages:** In many areas, there are water shortages as a result of increased demand brought on by overpopulation. This can aggravate issues with water by affecting industry, agriculture, and access to clean drinking water.

4. **Urbanisation Issues:** Overpopulation-induced rapid urbanisation can put a strain on the city's infrastructure and services. Problems like traffic jams, subpar housing, poor sanitation, and overcrowded public transit can occur.

5. **Health Problems:** Overcrowding in living conditions can facilitate the spread of infectious diseases. Access to healthcare may become difficult, and public health infrastructure may become insufficient to meet the needs of a large population.

6. **Poverty and Inequality:** Overpopulation can contribute to poverty, especially in resource-constrained areas. Unequal resource and opportunity distribution can exacerbate social and economic inequalities.

7. **Unemployment and Underemployment:** Rapid population growth can outpace job creation, resulting in high levels of unemployment or underemployment. This can lead to economic insecurity and social unrest.

8. Strain on Education Systems: Overpopulation can put a strain on educational systems, resulting in overcrowded classrooms, a shortage of qualified teachers, and insufficient educational resources. This can have an adverse effect on the quality of education provided.

9. Political and Social Instability: Societies experiencing overpopulation may experience political and social turbulence as a result of increased competition for resources, economic challenges, and strains on public services. This insecurity may have regional or global ramifications.

10. Increased Carbon Emissions: An increase in population often means an increase in energy consumption and carbon emissions, which contributes to climate change and environmental problems.

11. Loss of Arable Land: Population growth may result in the conversion of arable land for housing and infrastructure, reducing the available land for agriculture. This has the potential to have an impact on food production and food security.

12. Pressure on Ecosystems: Overpopulation can lead to the encroachment of human activities into natural ecosystems, disrupting ecosystem balance and leading to the loss of biodiversity.

Overpopulation problems frequently necessitate comprehensive and long-term solutions, such as education, family planning, resource management, and efforts to promote economic and social development. Sustainable solutions entail striking a balance between population size and the environment's ability to support it.

Controlling overpopulation requires a multifaceted and comprehensive approach that addresses the underlying causes while also incorporating strategies for long-term development. Several key strategies are as follows:

1. Promotion of Education:

• Education on Family Planning: Implement comprehensive education programmes focusing on family planning, reproductive health, and the benefits of smaller family sizes.

• Access to Quality Education: Increase access to quality education, particularly for women, because educated women have fewer children.

2. Providing Access to Family Planning Services:

• Affordability and Accessibility: Create and promote affordable and accessible family planning services, including contraception, in both urban and rural areas.

• Community Outreach: Hold community outreach programmes to raise awareness about the importance of family planning options.

3. Empowering Women:

• Gender Equality: Promote gender equality in all aspects of life, including education, employment, and decision-making, empowering women to make informed family planning decisions.

• Reproductive Rights: Women's reproductive rights must be advocated for and protected in order for them to have control over their reproductive health.

4. Economic Growth and Poverty Reduction:

• Job Creation: Enact policies and programmes that promote economic development and job creation in order to alleviate poverty and break the link between poverty and high birth rates.

• Microfinance and Entrepreneurship: Encourage microfinance initiatives and entrepreneurship programmes to economically empower individuals and families.

5. Policies and Incentives of the Government:

• Incentive Programmes: Implement incentive programmes for smaller families, such as tax breaks, healthcare benefits, or educational opportunities.

• Effective Legislation: Enforce and strengthen legislation supporting family planning, reproductive health, and women's rights.

6. Infrastructure for Healthcare:

• Improving Healthcare Access: Ensure access to maternal and child healthcare, as well as family planning services, by strengthening healthcare infrastructure.

• Preventive Healthcare: Prioritise preventive healthcare measures to lower infant mortality rates, which may influence family size decisions.

7. International Collaboration:

• Worldwide Cooperation: Encourage worldwide cooperation and collaboration on population control efforts, recognising that overpopulation is a global concern.

• Aid and Support: Assist developing countries in implementing effective population control strategies.

8. Innovations in Technology:

• Research and Development: Invest in research and development for new technologies that promote sustainable living, resource efficiency, and environmentally friendly practises.

• Technological Solutions: Use technology to support sustainable agriculture, renewable energy, and smart city planning.

9. Ethical Considerations:

• Human Rights Approach: Develop and implement population control strategies based on human rights, while respecting individuals' autonomy and choices.

• Community Involvement: Involve communities in decision-making processes while taking cultural and ethical perspectives into account.

10. Evaluation and Monitoring:

• Data Collection: Create robust data collection systems to monitor demographic trends, assess the efficacy of population control measures, and adjust policies as needed.

• Adaptability: Maintain your ability to adapt and respond to changing demographic patterns and emerging challenges.

11. Promoting Sustainable Ways of Life:

• Environmental Awareness: Promote environmental awareness and sustainable lifestyles in order to reduce the overall ecological footprint.

• Resource Administration: Responsible resource management and consumption patterns are encouraged.

12. Advocacy and the Media:

- Public Awareness Campaigns: Use media and advocacy campaigns to educate the public about the consequences of overpopulation and the advantages of population control measures.
- Involvement of Celebrities and Influencers: Harness the power of celebrities and influencers to raise awareness about family planning and population control.

Collaboration between governments, non-governmental organisations, international organisations, and local communities is required to implement these strategies. Societies can achieve a balance between population size and the capacity of the environment to support it by addressing the underlying causes and promoting sustainable development.

Underemployment:

Underemployment occurs when an individual is employed, but their employment is insufficient in terms of hours worked, skill utilisation, or income earned in comparison to their qualifications, abilities, and availability for full-time work. This is in contrast to unemployment, where people are not working at all.

The following are significant aspects of underemployment:

1. Inadequate Work Hours: Individuals may work part-time or on irregular schedules, failing to meet the standard full-time employment hours for their occupation.

2. Underutilization of Skills: Employees may find themselves in jobs where their skills and qualifications are not fully utilised. This can occur when people take on roles that do not correspond to their education or professional background.

3. Low Income or Job Insecurity: Underemployed people may earn wages that are insufficient to meet their financial needs or provide economic security. They may also face job insecurity due to temporary or precarious employment arrangements.

4. Misalignment between education and job requirements: Some people may have more education and qualifications than are required for the job they are currently doing. This is commonly referred to as "overqualification."

5. Involuntary Part-Time Work: Some people prefer full-time work but can only find part-time work. They are considered underemployed in such cases because they are willing and available to work more hours.

6. Seasonal or cyclical work: Workers in seasonal or cyclical industries may experience underemployment during off-seasons or economic downturns when demand for their skills or services decreases.

7. Having More Than One Job: Underemployment can also occur when people work multiple jobs to make ends meet, indicating a lack of sufficient income from a single source of employment.

8. Lack of Opportunities for Advancement: Some people may be stuck in positions with no opportunities for career advancement or professional development, leading to a sense of underutilization of skills and potential.

Underemployment affects not only individuals but also the economy as a whole. It can lead to decreased productivity, decreased job satisfaction and slowed economic growth. Furthermore, underemployed individuals may face difficulties meeting financial obligations and gaining access to benefits typically associated with full-time employment.

Measuring underemployment can be difficult because it takes into account not only the number of jobs available but also job quality, skill match, and income adequacy. Various indicators are frequently used by policymakers and economists to assess the extent of underemployment in a given population.

Underemployment can be caused by a number of factors and the causes tend to be complex and multifaceted. Here are some of the most common causes of underemployment:

1. **Economic Downturns:** During economic downturns or recessions, businesses may reduce hiring as well as working hours for existing employees, resulting in underemployment.

2. **Mismatched Skills:** A mismatch between the skills workers possess and the skills required by available jobs can contribute to underemployment. This situation frequently occurs when people are overqualified for the jobs they hold.

3. **Part-Time Employment Norms:** In some industries, part-time or temporary employment has become the norm, resulting in workers being unable to secure full-time positions.

4. **Automation and Technological Advances:** Automation and technological advancements can lead to job

displacement and render certain skills obsolete, resulting in a workforce with skills that are not in high demand.

5. Globalisation: Increased globalisation can result in job outsourcing and increased competition, affecting job availability and wages in specific industries.

6. Cyclical Industries: Industries subject to cyclical demand, such as construction or agriculture, may experience fluctuations in employment levels, resulting in underemployment during downturns.

7. Underdeveloped Job Markets: Individuals in underdeveloped job markets may face limited opportunities, and available jobs may not match their qualifications and skills.

8. Lack of Professional Advancement: A lack of opportunities for career advancement within an organisation can lead to underemployment, as workers may find themselves stuck in positions with no opportunity to advance.

9. Seasonal Work: Seasonal employment, which is common in industries such as tourism and agriculture, may result in periods of underemployment during the off-season.

10. Relocation Challenges: Individuals may face underemployment if they are unwilling or unable to relocate for job opportunities, especially if there are few options in their current location.

11. Discouraged Workers: Those who are unemployed for an extended period of time may give up on their job search and take on part-time or low-skill jobs.

12. Flexible Work Arrangements: Although some people find flexibility in work arrangements to be beneficial, if people are unintentionally working fewer hours than they would like, it may lead to underemployment.

13. Economic Policy and Regulation: Policies and regulations imposed by the government may also have an impact. Hiring decisions and employment availability may be impacted by minimum wage laws, labour market regulations, and other policies.

In order to pinpoint the precise causes of underemployment in a particular setting, a thorough examination of industry dynamics, labour market trends, and local and global economic conditions is necessary. A combination of macroeconomic policies, educational programmes, and techniques to match skills with job requirements in a labour market that is changing quickly are frequently used to address underemployment.

Numerous issues for people as individuals, as families, and as a society at large can result from underemployment. The following are some typical issues brought on by underemployment:

1. Financial Stress: Unemployed people frequently face financial difficulties because their earnings are insufficient to meet basic needs, resulting in economic insecurity and increased stress.

2. Reduced Job Satisfaction: Underemployed workers may feel unfulfilled as well as dissatisfied with their jobs, particularly if their skills are not fully utilised or if they are stuck in positions with limited opportunities for advancement.

3. Limited Career Development: Underemployment can stifle professional growth and advancement by denying individuals the opportunity to learn new skills or gain relevant experience in their field.

4. Inability to Meet Financial Obligations: Underemployed people may struggle to meet financial obligations such as rent or mortgage payments, healthcare costs, and educational costs. This can result in debt buildup and financial instability.

5. Effect on Mental Health: The stress and frustration associated with underemployment can have a negative impact on mental health, resulting in anxiety, depression, and a diminished sense of self-worth.

6. Erosion of Skill: There is a risk of skill erosion when individuals are unable to use their skills to their full potential. This may make it more difficult for them to obtain higher-level positions in the future.

7. Reliance on Multiple Jobs: Some underemployed people may need to work multiple jobs to make ends meet, resulting in a lack of work-life balance, increased stress, and potential health issues.

8. Effect on Family Life: Because of financial stress and increased work demands, underemployment can strain family relationships. It may also restrict parents' ability to provide for their children's needs and education.

9. Healthcare Difficulties: Underemployed people frequently lack access to employer-sponsored healthcare benefits, making it difficult to obtain necessary medical care and contributing to health disparities.

10. Reduced Consumer Spending: Underemployed individuals frequently have limited disposable income, which can contribute to decreased consumer spending. This, in turn, can have far-reaching economic consequences, affecting both businesses and overall economic growth.

11. Social Stigma: In some societies, underemployment is stigmatised, causing feelings of shame and embarrassment in individuals who may feel judged for not achieving their career goals.

12. Impact on Retirement Planning: Underemployment can limit people's ability to save for retirement, potentially leading to financial problems later in life.

13. Reduced Productivity: From a macroeconomic standpoint, underemployment can contribute to decreased overall productivity because workers may not be fully engaged or motivated in their roles.

Addressing underemployment necessitates a mix of policies and initiatives centred on economic development, education, job creation, and worker support. Strategies that promote a more dynamic and inclusive job market, improve skill development, and promote fair labour practises can all help to alleviate the problems associated with underemployment.

Overcoming underemployment necessitates a concerted effort on the part of individuals, government policies, and broader economic strategies. Here are some key strategies for addressing and overcoming underemployment:

1. Education and Professional Development:

• Continuous Learning: Encourage people to engage in continuous learning and skill development to improve their qualifications and adapt to changing job market demands.

• Training Programmes: Government and private organisations can offer training programmes to prepare people for in-demand jobs.

2. Job Hunting and Networking:

• Job Search Techniques: Provide resources and guidance on effective job search techniques, such as using online platforms, networking events, and professional associations.

• Networking Opportunities: Promote networking in order to broaden professional connections, learn about job opportunities, and gain insights into specific industries.

3. Entrepreneurship and Small Business Development:

• Entrepreneurial Support: Assist individuals in starting their own businesses through entrepreneurship programmes, mentorship, and access to small business loans.

• Fostering Innovation: Create an environment that promotes innovation and the development of new businesses, as well as opportunities for self-employment.

4. Workplace Flexibility:

• Encourage Flexibility: Advocate for flexible work arrangements, such as part-time, remote, or freelance work, to give people more options for balancing work and personal obligations.

5. Government Policies and Legislation:

• Labour Market Policies: Develop and implement policies that promote fair labour practises, job security, and equal opportunity for workers.

• Subsidised Employment Programmes: Implement programmes that encourage businesses to hire more workers, particularly during economic downturns.

6. Economic Diversification:

• Diversifying Industries: Encourage economic diversification by investing in industries with high growth potential, resulting in a more resilient job market.

7. Assistance with Career Transitions:

• Career Counselling Services: Offer career counselling services to individuals to assist them in exploring new career paths and identifying transferable skills.

• Reskilling and Retraining Programmes: Create programmes to help workers transition from declining industries to sectors with higher demand.

8. Encouragement of Inclusive Hiring Practises:

• Anti-Discrimination Policies: Enforce anti-discrimination policies to ensure fair and inclusive hiring practises.

• Diversity and Inclusion Programmes: Encourage businesses to implement diversity and inclusion programmes in order to promote a diverse workforce.

9. Government Aid Programmes:

• Unemployment Benefits: Strengthen unemployment benefit programmes to provide a safety net for people who have lost their jobs or are working fewer hours.

• Training Subsidies: Subsidise training programmes to make them more accessible to unemployed people looking to advance their careers.

10. Encourage Remote Work:

• Remote Work Opportunities: Encourage businesses to offer remote work options, expanding the pool of available job opportunities to people who may face geographical constraints.

11. Community Support:

• Community Programmes: Create local community programmes that provide support, resources, and networking opportunities for people who are unemployed.

12. Advocacy and Awareness:

• Public Awareness Campaigns: Conduct public awareness campaigns about the challenges of underemployment and advocate for supportive policies at the local and national levels.

13. Social Innovation:

• Supporting Social Enterprises: Encourage the growth of social enterprises that aim to address societal challenges by creating jobs with a positive social impact.

14. Wellness Programmes in the Workplace:

• Wellness Initiatives: Promote workplace wellness programmes to support employees' mental and physical well-being, thereby increasing job satisfaction and productivity.

Individuals, employers, educational institutions, and policymakers must all work together to overcome underemployment. Societies can work to reduce the challenges associated with underemployment by fostering a dynamic and inclusive job market, providing support for skill development, and creating opportunities for career advancement.

Now, consider the interactions between overpopulation and underemployment:

1. Vicious Cycle: Overpopulation may exacerbate underemployment as the labour market struggles to absorb the growing workforce.

2. Economic Imbalance: In some cases, high population density can result in a surplus of low-skilled workers, contributing to underemployment and wage suppression.

3. Education and Family Planning: Addressing both issues necessitates a multifaceted approach. Improving education and encouraging family planning can help to reduce overpopulation and underemployment.

4. Innovation and Automation: Technological advancements and automation can help alleviate underemployment by creating new job opportunities; however, they may also contribute to job displacement in the short term.

5. Government Policies: Addressing these issues requires effective government policies. Policies that promote sustainable development, education, and workforce training can help to improve the situation.

To summarise, addressing overpopulation and underemployment necessitates a multifaceted approach that takes into account social, economic, and environmental factors. Any effective solution must include sustainable development, education, and strategic policymaking.

The Subconscious Mind and It's Power

For centuries, scholars, psychologists, and individuals have been fascinated by the concept of the subconscious mind. It represents an enigmatic realm within our psyche that is responsible for various aspects of our thoughts, feelings, and behaviours that occur outside of conscious awareness. This article delves into the world of the subconscious mind, investigating its nature, functions, and profound impact on human cognition and behaviour.

In order to understand the subconscious mind, it is necessary to first comprehend the human mind and its levels:

The mind is a central and multifaceted aspect of human cognition and consciousness. It represents the intricate interplay of an individual's inner world, which consists of thoughts, emotions, perceptions, memories, and mental processes. While different perspectives and theories exist on the nature of the mind, it can be broadly defined as follows:

The mind is the sum of a person's cognitive processes, which include conscious and subconscious elements. It is the centre of mental activity, where data is processed, stored, and synthesised. The mind is in charge of shaping a person's experiences, thoughts, beliefs, and emotions.

The following are key components of the mind:

1. Conscious Awareness: The conscious mind is made up of the thoughts, sensations, and perceptions that we are currently aware of. It enables us to think deliberately, make decisions, and solve problems. This aspect of the mind is commonly associated with our everyday experiences and self-awareness.

2. Subconscious Processes: The subconscious mind exists beneath the surface of conscious awareness, where a vast array of mental processes take place without our active attention. Memory storage and retrieval are examples of automatic behaviours, habits, and processes.

3. Thoughts and Cognitive Functions: The mind is the locus of thought processes such as reasoning, judgement, creativity, and problem-solving. These cognitive functions help us navigate the world, make decisions, and adapt to changing conditions.

4. Emotions and Feelings: Emotions and feelings are also stored in the mind and influence our perceptions and responses to the world around us. Emotional states like happiness, fear and sadness are essential to the human experience.

5. Memory: Memory is one of the fundamental functions of the "mind." It entails the storage and retrieval of information, allowing us to learn from our experiences, recall past events, and expand our knowledge.

6. Perception: Our subjective experience of reality is created by the mind's interpretation of sensory input from the external world. This includes our perceptions of what we see, hear, taste, smell, and touch.

7. Beliefs and Values: Our beliefs, values, and worldviews are shaped by our minds, and they guide our thoughts, actions, and decisions. These deeply held beliefs shape our behaviour and interactions with others.

8. Consciousness: The mind is inextricably linked to consciousness, the state of being aware of and responsive to one's surroundings. Consciousness enables us to experience life and contemplate our existence.

9. Imagination and Creativity: The mind fosters imagination and creativity, allowing us to imagine new possibilities, generate ideas, and engage in artistic and innovative endeavours.

10. Sense of Self: The mind plays a vital role in the development of an individual's sense of self and identity. It contains one's life story, self-concept, and personal history.

The study of the mind is a multidisciplinary field that includes psychology, neuroscience, philosophy, and cognitive science. It seeks to comprehend the complexities of mental processes, consciousness mechanisms, and the nature of subjective experience.

To summarise, the mind is the focal point of human cognition, encompassing conscious and subconscious processes, emotions, thoughts, memories, and perceptions. It is the intricate web of mental activities that collectively define and mould an individual's inner world and life experience.

The conscious mind and the unconscious mind are the two most important components of human cognition and mental processes. The accessibility, content, and influence on behaviour of these two aspects of the mind differ in a variety of ways. The following are the key distinctions between the conscious mind and the unconscious mind:

1. Conscious Awareness vs. Lack of Awareness:

• **Conscious Mind:** This is the aspect of the mind associated with awareness. It includes thoughts, perceptions, and mental processes that an individual is currently aware of. It entails deliberate reasoning, thinking, and decision-making.

• **Unconscious Mind:** The unconscious mind is made up of mental processes that occur without conscious awareness. These processes take place beneath the surface of conscious thought and are inaccessible for conscious scrutiny.

2. Accessibility:

• **Conscious Mind:** An individual's conscious mind is directly accessible and controllable. It enables us to actively concentrate on and control our thoughts and mental activities.

• **Unconscious Mind:** Typically, the unconscious mind is not directly accessible to conscious control. It operates autonomously and frequently escapes conscious scrutiny. Accessing and comprehending unconscious processes frequently necessitates the use of specialised techniques such as therapy, meditation, or self-reflection.

3. Information and Processing:

• **Conscious Mind:** Information is processed in a linear and sequential manner by the conscious mind. Individuals engage in logical reasoning, critical thinking, and deliberate decision-making in this setting. It is the domain of conscious thoughts and awareness.

• **Unconscious Mind:** Information is processed by the unconscious mind in a parallel, associative, and holistic manner. It is the site of implicit, automatic, and emotional processes. It addresses memory, emotions, habits, and automatic behaviours.

4. Limited Processing Capacity:

• **Conscious Mind:** The conscious mind has a limited processing capacity. It can only concentrate on a few pieces of data or tasks at a time. Multitasking within the conscious mind can be difficult because it necessitates cognitive resources.

• **Unconscious Mind:** The unconscious mind has an enormous and largely limitless processing capacity. It can manage a variety of background tasks at the same time, such as regulating bodily functions, processing sensory information, and managing learned behaviours.

5. Self-awareness and Awareness of the External World:

• **Conscious Mind:** The conscious mind is where people experience self-awareness and a direct connection to the outside world. It is the location of conscious perceptions, self-reflection, and introspection.

• **Unconscious Mind:** The unconscious mind is not synonymous with self-awareness. It is in charge of processes that do not require immediate attention and operates largely outside of conscious awareness.

6. Influence on Behaviour:

• **Conscious Mind:** The conscious mind plays an important role in shaping intentional behaviours and choices. It is the place where people make conscious decisions and exercise willpower.

• **The Unconscious Mind:** The unconscious mind has a significant influence on behaviour, often in subtle ways. It is capable of causing automatic behaviours, emotional responses, and the expression of habits and learned patterns.

7. Information Storage:

• **Conscious Mind:** The conscious mind stores a limited amount of information for immediate use. It serves as a setting for active cognitive processes.

• **Unconscious Mind:** The unconscious mind is in charge of long-term memory, emotion, and learned behaviour storage. It stores information and experiences that may be difficult to recall consciously.

Understanding the distinctions between the conscious and unconscious mind is essential for understanding human cognition, behaviour, and the mechanisms underlying decision-making and emotional responses. These two aspects of the mind collaborate to shape our perceptions, thoughts, and actions.

A table illustrating the key distinctions between the conscious and unconscious minds:

Aspect	Conscious Mind	Unconscious Mind
Awareness	Associated with awareness and conscious thought.	Operates without conscious awareness.
Accessibility	Directly accessible and controllable.	Typically not directly accessible or controllable.
Content and Processing	Linear and sequential processing of	Parallel, associative, and holistic processing.

	information.	
Limited Processing Capacity	Can focus on a limited number of tasks.	Vast and unlimited processing capacity.
Awareness of Self and the External World	Involves self-awareness and perception of the external world.	Lacks self-awareness and operates beyond conscious awareness.
Influence on Behavior	Shapes deliberate behaviors and choices.	Drives automatic behaviors, emotions, and habits.
Storage of Information	Stores a limited amount of information for short-term use.	Responsible for long-term storage of memories and learned behaviors.

This table compares the conscious and unconscious minds in terms of awareness, accessibility, processing, and their roles in shaping human behaviour and cognition.

Another important aspect of the mind is the subconscious mind. Let us go over it in more detail:

The concept of the subconscious mind dates back to the late nineteenth and early twentieth centuries, with key figures such as Sigmund Freud and Carl Jung playing pivotal roles in its evolution. The "unconscious" was introduced by Freud as a repository of repressed desires and memories that influence human behaviour. Jung developed this idea further by proposing a "collective unconscious," or a shared reservoir of archetypal symbols and experiences.

The subconscious mind, which is frequently used interchangeably with the unconscious, refers to mental processes that take place just below the threshold of consciousness, including automatic behaviours, habits, and the processing of information that is not immediately visible. While the conscious mind is responsible for immediate awareness, decision-making, and logical reasoning, the unconscious and subconscious minds are critical in automatic processing, memory storage, and shaping long-term behaviours, beliefs, and emotional responses.

The subconscious mind performs several vital tasks that have a significant impact on our daily lives and behaviour:

1. Information Processing in the Subconscious Mind:

The human mind is a complex and multifaceted entity, with various levels and processes that work in harmony to enable cognition and behaviour. One of the most fascinating and enigmatic components of the mind is the subconscious mind, which plays a pivotal role in information processing.

We will delve into the workings of the subconscious mind, its capacity for information processing, and how it influences our thoughts, emotions, and actions in this comprehensive exploration.

I. An Overview of the Subconscious Mind

The subconscious mind is a psychological concept that refers to the part of the mind that operates below the level of conscious awareness. It is a vast repository of knowledge, experiences, beliefs, and memories that shape our lives. Unlike the conscious mind, which is concerned with immediate perceptions and decisions, the subconscious mind is concerned with a wide range of processes that frequently occur in the background.

A. Automatic Information Processing

The ability of the subconscious mind to automatically process information is one of its most prominent functions. This includes a wide range of activities such as physiological function regulation, sensory input filtering, and behavioural management. It monitors vital functions such as heart rate, digestion, and breathing, for example, without requiring conscious effort.

B. Memory Storage

The subconscious mind is a storage place for memories and experiences. It saves information from our past, including not only facts but also emotional associations. These memories are frequently inaccessible to conscious recall, but they can have a significant impact on our thoughts, emotions, and behaviours.

C. Beliefs and Value Systems

Our subconscious mind is where our core beliefs, values, and attitudes are formed and maintained. These beliefs influence our self-image and play an important role in shaping our decision-making processes. These aspects are rooted in the subconscious, whether we believe in our abilities, have a positive or negative self-concept, or hold particular political or religious beliefs.

D. Automatic Behaviour and Emotional Reactions

The subconscious mind is in charge of initiating automatic responses, habits, and emotional reactions. These responses are frequently influenced by previous experiences and can influence our behaviour without our conscious participation. A traumatic childhood experience, for example, may cause subconscious anxiety that influences our adult decision-making and emotional reactions.

E. Problem Solving

The subconscious mind also solves problems and thinks creatively. It has an amazing ability to work on problems in the background, which frequently results in "Eureka!" moments when solutions and insights suddenly emerge into conscious awareness. Throughout history, artists, scientists, and thinkers have attributed their creative ideas to the workings of the subconscious mind.

II. How the Subconscious Mind Processes Information

To comprehend the mechanics of information processing in the subconscious mind, it is necessary to investigate some key principles and processes:

A. Filtering Sensory Input

Only a subset of sensory input is processed by the subconscious mind, allowing only a subset of information to reach conscious awareness. This filtering mechanism allows us to focus on what is most important at any given time and keeps our brains from being overwhelmed by the sheer volume of sensory data they receive.

B. Memory Consolidation

Memory consolidation is an important aspect of information processing in the subconscious mind. Information is transferred from short-term memory to long-term memory during this process. It occurs frequently during sleep, particularly during the rapid eye movement (REM) stage, and is required for the formation of long-term memories. The subconscious mind assesses the significance of information and determines which experiences should be saved for future use.

C. Recognising Patterns

The subconscious mind's fundamental role is pattern recognition. It enables us to distinguish between similar and dissimilar stimuli, experiences, and situations. Because of our ability to recognise patterns, we can make quick judgements and decisions based on prior learning and knowledge.

D. Neural Pathways

Neural pathways are important in information processing because they connect different levels of consciousness. These pathways facilitate information transfer between the conscious and subconscious realms. When information is transferred from the subconscious to the conscious mind, it has the potential to influence our thoughts, emotions, and behaviours.

E. Emotional Connections

Emotions and information processing in the subconscious mind are inextricably linked. Emotional associations with memories and experiences frequently shape our reactions and decisions. For example, a person who had a happy childhood may form a positive emotional association with the concept of family, influencing their beliefs and decisions about starting their own family.

F. Mental Imagery and Visualisation

Mental imagery and visualisation are used by the subconscious mind to process information. It can generate and manipulate mental images that can be used for problem solving, creativity, and planning. Techniques such as visualisation and imagery can tap into this aspect of the subconscious, facilitating goal achievement and skill improvement.

III. Accessing and Harnessing the Subconscious Mind's Information Processing Abilities

While the subconscious mind processes information automatically, we can gain access to it and influence how it works. Here are some methods for harnessing its information processing abilities:

A. Meditation and Mindfulness

Meditation and mindfulness practises are powerful tools for bringing subconscious thoughts and emotions to the surface of conscious awareness. Individuals can become more attuned to their inner world and gain insight into their thought patterns and emotional responses by engaging in these practises.

B. Keep a Journal

Keeping a journal can be an extremely effective tool for exploring the subconscious mind. Writing down your thoughts, feelings, and dreams can help you discover patterns and hidden beliefs that may influence your behaviour. It offers a structured method of accessing and processing subconscious information.

C. Introspection

Self-reflection and introspection on a regular basis help people become more aware of their subconscious motivations and beliefs. This increased self-awareness is a critical step towards making conscious changes in response to subconscious mind information.

D. Therapy

Psychotherapy, particularly modalities such as psychoanalysis and cognitive-behavioral therapy, provides individuals with a structured and guided approach to exploring and addressing the contents of the subconscious mind. Therapists assist clients in discovering and resolving hidden issues and beliefs that may be influencing their lives.

E. Expression of Creativity

Art, music, writing, and dance are examples of creative activities that provide an outlet for subconscious thoughts and emotions. Individuals can use creative expression to express and process their inner world in a therapeutic and transformative way.

IV. The Subconscious Mind and Cognitive Science

Modern cognitive science and neuroscience have made significant advances in deciphering the mysteries of the subconscious mind and its information processing. These breakthroughs have provided important insights into how the brain manages and influences conscious and subconscious aspects of thought.

A. Neural Correlates of the Subconscious Mind

Neuroscientists have identified several brain regions associated with subconscious processes. For example, the amygdala is important in processing emotions and forming emotional memories that are stored in the subconscious.

B. Sleep and Memory Processing

Sleep, especially the REM stage, plays a vital role for memory consolidation. During sleep, the subconscious mind assesses the importance of information and decides what to store in long-term memory. The link between sleep and memory consolidation emphasises the importance of the subconscious mind in learning and memory consolidation.

C. Cognitive Biases and Heuristics

The subconscious mind frequently uses cognitive heuristics and biases, such as availability heuristic and confirmation bias, as cognitive short cuts when processing information. While these shortcuts can save time, they can also lead to mistakes in judgement and decision-making.

D. Unconscious Priming

Unconscious priming is a phenomenon in which exposure to certain stimuli influences subsequent thoughts, emotions, and behaviours without the individual's conscious knowledge. While these shortcuts can save time, they can also lead to mistakes in judgement and decision-making.

V. Moral and Ethical Considerations

Understanding the complexities of the subconscious mind and its information processing abilities raises significant moral and ethical concerns.

VI. Conclusion

Understanding the complexities of information processing in the subconscious mind sheds light on the subtle yet profound ways it shapes our experiences. The filtering, storage, and automatic processing of information all contribute to the smooth operation of our cognitive processes. While the subconscious mind operates largely outside of conscious awareness, its influence pervades many aspects of our lives, making it a fascinating area of study in the field of psychology.

2. Memory Storage in the Subconscious Mind:

Memory is a fundamental component of human cognition, shaping our perception of the world and our place in it. Memory is not a single entity; it is made up of numerous systems and processes. Memory's storage in the subconscious mind, where a variety of experiences, knowledge, and emotions are preserved, is an essential component. We will delve into the complexities of memory storage in the subconscious mind, its mechanisms, and how it influences our thoughts, emotions, and behaviours in this in-depth exploration.

I. Memory Storage and the Subconscious Mind

In psychology, the subconscious mind refers to the part of the mind that operates below the level of conscious awareness. It is essential for storing, processing, and influencing memories. This hidden storehouse of experiences, knowledge, and emotions serves as the backdrop for how we interpret and navigate our conscious lives.

A. Automatic Memory Storage

The automatic storage of memories is one of the most significant roles of the subconscious mind. These memories cover a wide range of experiences, from mundane to profound. The subconscious mind, in contrast to the conscious mind, which selectively retains a limited amount of information, stores a vast and continuous stream of experiences over the course of a lifetime.

B. Emotional Connections

Subconscious memories are frequently associated with emotional connections. These emotional connections can be both explicit and implicit, colouring our memories of the past and influencing our emotional reactions in the present. A childhood memory of a favourite family vacation, for example, may be associated with positive emotional associations, eliciting feelings of nostalgia and happiness when recalled.

C. Unconscious Memories

Many memories stored in the subconscious mind are not easily recalled by conscious thought. These are oftentimes referred to as unconscious memories. They may be forgotten or repressed for a time, but they continue to shape our thoughts, emotions, and behaviours.

D. The Influence on Conscious Experience

Memories stored in the subconscious mind have a significant impact on our conscious experience. They can influence our perceptions, attitudes, and decisions without our knowledge. For example, a person who has a subconscious memory of a traumatic event in the past may experience increased anxiety in situations reminiscent of that event, even if they cannot recall the trauma consciously.

II. Memory Storage Mechanisms in the Subconscious Mind

To comprehend the mechanics of memory storage in the subconscious mind, it is crucial to look into some key mechanisms and processes:

A. Encoding and Retrieval

Encoding is the process by which information from the outside world is transformed into a format suitable for storage. Memories can be retrieved once they have been encoded. Various cognitive processes and neural activity aid in encoding and retrieval, with the subconscious mind playing a key role in both phases.

B. Memory Consolidation

Memory consolidation is the process of transferring information from short-term memory to long-term memory. This happens a lot during sleep, especially during the rapid eye movement (REM) stage. The subconscious mind assesses the importance of information and determines which experiences should be saved for future use.

C. Storage of Emotional Memories

The subconscious mind excels at storing memories with strong emotional content. Emotions, whether positive or negative, can enhance memory consolidation. Emotional memories are more vivid and long-lasting, and they frequently play an important role in our lives, shaping our responses and behaviours.

D. Hierarchy of Memory Storage

Memories stored in the subconscious mind are frequently organised in a hierarchical order based on factors such as emotional significance and relevance. Some memories are easily retrieved, whereas others are stored deeper in the subconscious and may require specific triggers or associations to be retrieved.

E. Memory Connections

Memories in the subconscious mind are linked together by a web of associations. When a specific memory is recalled, it can cause related memories to be retrieved. These associative links may explain why a single recollection can trigger a flood of related memories, adding to the richness and complexity of our internal landscape.

III. Accessing Memories in the Subconscious Mind

While many memories are stored in the subconscious mind and are therefore hidden from conscious awareness, there are methods for accessing and retrieving them. Individuals can explore their hidden memories using the following techniques and approaches:

A. Psychotherapy

Psychotherapy, particularly modalities such as psychoanalysis, focuses on exploring and resolving unconscious memories and their associated emotional content. Therapists assist people in delving into their subconscious minds in order to uncover and process repressed memories and unresolved issues.

B. Dream Interpretation

Dreams provide a direct glimpse into the subconscious mind. Dream analysis can reveal hidden memories, unresolved conflicts, and emotional associations. Certain dream symbols and themes may allude to more profound subconscious content.

C. Hypnosis

Hypnosis is a state of focused attention and relaxation that allows access to the subconscious mind. Individuals may recall past events and memories that were previously beyond their conscious reach while under hypnosis.

D. Mindfulness and Meditation

Mindfulness and meditation are two practises that can help people become more aware of their inner world and access hidden memories. These practises can bring submerged memories to the surface by calming the conscious mind and encouraging introspection.

IV. The Subconscious Mind, Memory and Cognitive Science

Modern cognitive science and neuroscience have made significant progress in unravelling the mysteries of subconscious memory storage. These breakthroughs provide important insights into how the brain manages and influences memory and conscious thought.

A. Neural Correlates of Memory Storage

Memory storage is associated with specific brain regions and neural pathways, according to neuroscientists. The hippocampus, for instance, plays a vital role for memory formation and retrieval. As an integral part of the cognitive system, the subconscious mind is inextricably linked to these neural processes.

B. Retrieval and Recall of Memories

Memory retrieval is a complicated process that includes both conscious and subconscious components. By activating associative connections and providing emotional context to the recalled information, the subconscious mind aids in memory retrieval.

C. The Importance of Sleep

Sleep, especially the REM stage, is critical for memory consolidation and memory storage in the subconscious mind. During sleep, the brain reviews and evaluates information, deciding what should be stored in long-term memory.

D. Repression and Memory Recovery

The phenomenon of repressed memories is inextricably linked with the subconscious mind. Because of their emotionally charged or traumatic nature, repressed memories have been unconsciously blocked from conscious awareness. In some cases, therapeutic approaches can help to recover repressed memories and bring them back into conscious awareness.

V. Moral and Ethical Considerations

The study of memory storage in the subconscious mind raises significant ethical and moral issues, particularly in the context of repressed memories and their potential recovery. Memory retrieval must be done responsibly and with consideration for the emotional well-being of the individuals involved.

VI. Conclusion

Memory storage in the subconscious mind is a fascinating and complex aspect of human cognition. It is a dynamic process that influences our thoughts, emotions, and behaviours. Understanding the mechanisms and operation of memory storage in the subconscious mind can lead to personal development, self-discovery, and the resolution of unresolved issues. It emphasises the intricate interplay between conscious and subconscious aspects of our mental lives, as well as the breadth and depth of human memory.

3. Belief Systems in the Subconscious Mind:

Belief systems are an important part of human psychology because they influence our perceptions, behaviours, and decision-making. These belief systems do not exist only in conscious thought; they are deeply embedded in the subconscious mind. We will delve into the complexities of belief systems in the subconscious mind, their formation, impact on our lives, and methods for understanding and influencing them in this comprehensive exploration.

I. An Overview of Belief Systems

Belief systems are a complex web of interconnected ideas, values, attitudes, and convictions that shape and guide our behaviour. They are not limited to religious or spiritual beliefs, but include a wide range of concepts such as self-beliefs, societal beliefs, political ideologies, and moral values.

A. Conscious and Subconscious Beliefs

Beliefs are divided into two categories: conscious and subconscious. Conscious beliefs are those that we are aware of and can articulate. Subconscious beliefs, on the other hand, exist beneath the surface of conscious thought and are frequently more difficult to access and comprehend.

B. The Role of Beliefs

Beliefs are crucial in human cognition and behaviour. They function as mental frameworks that assist us in making sense of the world, interpreting experiences, and making decisions. Beliefs shape our emotions, shape our perceptions, and drive our actions.

II. Belief System Formation in the Subconscious Mind

The subconscious mind's belief systems evolve over time as a result of a combination of experiences, influences, and cognitive processes. Understanding how these beliefs form is critical to understanding their impact on our lives.

A. Early Childhood Experiences

Many subconscious beliefs have their origins in early childhood experiences. We are highly impressionable during these formative years and absorb information from our family, carers, and immediate environment. During this time, many people develop beliefs about their own worth, safety, and relationships.

B. Influences of Culture and Society

The larger cultural and societal context in which we grow up has a significant impact on the formation of our belief systems. Cultural norms, values, and expectations are absorbed and become deeply ingrained in our subconscious. These beliefs include ideas about gender, race, social roles, and societal structures.

C. Personal Experiences

Personal experiences, whether positive or negative, can influence the formation of beliefs in the subconscious mind. Traumatic events, achievements, and significant life transitions can all have a long-term impact on our beliefs about ourselves, the world, and our abilities.

D. Education and Learning

Education and learning have an impact on the formation of belief systems. Formal education, exposure to different points of view, and knowledge acquisition all contribute to expand or reinforce existing beliefs. The subconscious mind is open to new experiences and adapts accordingly.

E. Reinforcement and Socialisation

Beliefs in the subconscious mind are frequently reinforced through socialisation and interactions with peers and authority figures. These social influences have the potential to perpetuate certain belief systems and encourage conformity to societal norms.

III. The Influence of Belief Systems in the Subconscious Mind

The subconscious mind's beliefs have a significant impact on our lives. They have a subtle and automatic influence on various aspects of our thoughts, emotions, and behaviours.

A. Self-Image and Self-Worth

Subconscious belief systems have a significant impact on our self-image and self-worth. Positive beliefs about one's abilities and self-worth can foster self-confidence and resilience, whereas negative beliefs can lead to self-doubt and insecurity.

B. Decision-Making

Beliefs are vital in decision-making. They serve as benchmarks against which options are measured. Subconscious beliefs can influence decisions, causing them to align with existing belief systems.

C. Emotional Reactions

Emotions and subconscious beliefs are inextricably linked. Emotional reactions can be triggered by beliefs about oneself, others, and the world. When faced with a difficult task, a subconscious belief in one's incompetence may cause anxiety and self-criticism.

D. Perceptions and Interpretations

The subconscious mind's belief systems filter our perceptions and interpretations of events and experiences. They can result in cognitive biases, which influence how we perceive the world and the people around us.

E. Behaviour and Habits

Behaviour and habits are guided by subconscious beliefs. Beliefs can either support or obstruct the development of specific behaviours, such as healthy lifestyle choices, risk-taking, or interpersonal interactions.

F. Coping and Resilience

Beliefs influence how people deal with adversity and challenges. Individuals who are resilient frequently have subconscious beliefs that encourage perseverance and problem-solving, whereas those who have less adaptive beliefs may struggle to cope effectively.

IV. Understanding and Influencing Subconscious Belief Systems

Understanding and influencing the subconscious mind's belief systems is a process that can lead to personal growth and transformation. To access and modify these beliefs, several strategies can be used:

A. Self-Reflection

Self-reflection entails introspection and an examination of one's own belief systems. Individuals can gain insight into the origins of their convictions and assess their relevance to their lives by questioning and examining them.

B. Keep a journal

Keeping a journal can be an effective way to uncover subconscious beliefs. Writing about one's thoughts, feelings, and experiences can reveal patterns and underlying beliefs that influence behaviour.

C. Psychotherapy

Psychotherapy, particularly cognitive-behavioral therapy (CBT), assists individuals in exploring and challenging subconscious beliefs. Therapists assist clients in identifying and replacing negative or irrational beliefs with more adaptive ones.

D. Mindfulness and Meditation

Mindfulness and meditation practises can help you become more aware of your subconscious beliefs and how they affect your thoughts and emotions. Individuals can identify and assess their belief systems by remaining present and observing their inner world.

E. Affirmations

Affirmations are positive statements or beliefs that are repeated to counteract negative or unhelpful subconscious convictions. Affirmations, when used consistently, can lead to the reprogramming of belief systems over time.

F. Visualisation

Visualisation techniques use the power of the imagination to change subconscious beliefs. Individuals can influence their belief systems and behaviour by vividly imagining positive outcomes and scenarios.

G. Exposure to New Experiences

Exposure to a variety of experiences, people and ideas have the potential to challenge and expand existing belief systems. Interacting with people from different backgrounds or participating in new activities can cause subconscious beliefs to shift.

V. Moral and Ethical Considerations

Exploring and influencing subconscious belief systems raises ethical and moral concerns, particularly in a therapeutic context. Approaching belief system modification with sensitivity and respect for individual autonomy and cultural differences is critical. Individuals and therapists must be aware of potential ethical issues and ensure that the process is carried out responsibly and ethically.

VI. Conclusion

The subconscious mind's belief systems are an intricate tapestry of ideas and convictions that shape our perceptions, emotions, and actions. They are deeply ingrained in our individual experiences, cultural context, and socialisation. Understanding and influencing these belief systems is a valuable tool for personal development and self-improvement. We can choose to embrace or modify our subconscious beliefs that underpin our thoughts and behaviours by becoming aware of them. This leads to a more conscious and intentional way of living. Individuals can transform their lives and align their beliefs with their aspirations and values by consciously shaping their subconscious belief systems.

4. Influence on Behaviour in the Subconscious Mind:

The human mind is a complex and multifaceted entity, with conscious and subconscious processes working in tandem to shape behaviour. The subconscious mind, which operates beneath the surface of conscious awareness, is crucial in influencing our actions, decisions, and habits. We will delve into the intricate ways in which the subconscious mind influences human behaviour, the mechanisms underlying this influence, and strategies for better understanding and harnessing its power in this comprehensive exploration.

I. The Subconscious Mind:

In psychology, the subconscious mind refers to the part of the mind that operates below the level of conscious awareness. It contains a vast reservoir of information, memories, emotions, and beliefs that have a significant impact on our daily lives. While the conscious mind is in charge of rational thought and decision-making, the subconscious mind operates in the background, frequently influencing behaviour without our awareness.

A. Automatic Responses and Behaviour

Automatic responses and habits are two of the most prominent ways in which the subconscious mind influences behaviour. These automatic behaviours are typically learned over time and executed automatically. They can include anything from simple motor skills to complex social behaviours.

B. Memory and Experience

The subconscious mind is a storehouse of memories and experiences, and these memories can influence behaviour. Positive and negative past experiences influence our actions by providing a foundation for decision-making and steering us away from potential risks and towards familiar, safe alternatives.

C. Emotions and Emotional Regulation

Emotions are inextricably linked to the subconscious mind. Subconscious thoughts, memories, and beliefs can elicit emotions that are often unnoticed. These emotions have a significant impact on our behaviour because they guide our reactions to various situations.

D. Values and Beliefs

Many of our fundamental beliefs, values, and attitudes are stored in our subconscious minds. These deeply ingrained beliefs shape our self-concept and moral compass, directing our behaviour based on our internal value system. A person who subconsciously values honesty, for example, is more likely to act truthfully even in difficult situations.

II. Mechanisms of Influence

It is essential to investigate several key processes in order to comprehend the mechanisms by which the subconscious mind influences behaviour:

A. Formation of Habits

The subconscious mind influences behaviour primarily through habits. Habits are formed by repeatedly repeating a specific behaviour until it becomes automatic. Once a habit is formed, the subconscious mind takes over, resulting in behaviour that does not require conscious decision-making.

B. Emotion-Driven Behaviour

Emotions play an important role in behaviour, and the subconscious mind frequently triggers emotional responses based on previous experiences and beliefs. A traumatic past event, for example, can cause subconscious fear, influencing future decisions and behaviours to avoid similar situations.

C. Recall of Memories

The subconscious mind accesses memories that have been stored over time, and these memories frequently influence current behaviour. The recall of a previous experience or knowledge can guide current decision-making and actions. For example, a person may avoid a particular food subconsciously due to a previous negative experience with it.

D. Recognition of Patterns

The subconscious mind is skilled at identifying patterns and associations. It detects similarities and differences in a variety of situations and employs this knowledge to influence behaviour. For example, if a person has had positive experiences in team environments, they are more likely to gravitate towards group activities because their subconscious recognises the positive pattern.

E. Emotional Associations

Emotional associations play an important role in the subconscious influence on behaviour. These associations connect specific behaviours, situations, or decisions to specific emotions. For example, if a person associates public speaking with anxiety, the subconscious mind may trigger anxiety in similar situations, influencing the person's behaviour.

F. Implicit Memory

Implicit memory is a type of memory that operates independently of conscious awareness. It includes procedural memory, which guides motor skills and actions, as well as priming, which occurs when a stimulus is exposed and influences subsequent behaviour. Without conscious involvement, subconscious processes involved in implicit memory significantly shape behaviour.

III. The Subconscious Mind's Influence on Behaviour

The subconscious mind has significant influence over behaviour, often in ways that the individual is unaware of. Understanding this power is necessary for personal development and self-improvement.

A. Habitual Behaviour

Habits, which are the result of the subconscious mind, play an important role in daily behaviour. Whether it's the habit of checking your phone first thing in the morning or the habit of exercising regularly, the subconscious mind effortlessly guides these behaviours.

B. Emotional Responses

Subconscious emotions can have a significant impact on behaviour. Subconscious fear, for example, can lead to avoidance behaviour, whereas subconscious love can motivate people to connect with others and form relationships.

C. Decision Making

Even when we believe our choices are based on rational thought, the subconscious mind frequently participates in decision making processes. It processes information, including memories and beliefs, and aids in the evaluation of options in order to make decisions that are consistent with our internal values and experiences.

D. Creativity and Problem Solving

The subconscious mind is a powerhouse of creativity and problem solving. It processes information in the background, connecting seemingly unrelated concepts. This process has the potential to yield insights and novel solutions to complex problems.

E. Intuition and Gut Feelings

The ability of the subconscious mind to process large amounts of information quickly can be attributed to intuition or gut feelings. It provides quick insights and judgements based on subconscious patterns and associations.

IV. Accessing and Understanding the Subconscious Mind

Accessing and comprehending the subconscious mind is a time-consuming and ongoing process. Several techniques and approaches can aid in this investigation:

A. Meditation and Mindfulness

Meditation and mindfulness practises can bring unconscious thoughts and emotions to the surface of consciousness. Individuals can access their inner world and gain insight into their thought patterns and emotions by calming the conscious mind and focusing on the present moment.

B. Keep a journal

A journal is an effective tool for exploring the subconscious mind. Writing down your thoughts, emotions, and dreams can help you discover patterns and hidden beliefs that can influence your behaviour. It offers a structured method of accessing and processing subconscious information.

C. Therapy

Psychotherapy provides people with a structured and guided way to explore and address the contents of their subconscious minds. Therapists assist clients in identifying and resolving hidden issues and beliefs that may be affecting their lives.

D. Creative Expression

Art, music, writing, and dance are examples of creative activities that provide an outlet for subconscious thoughts and emotions. Individuals can use creative expression to express and process their inner world in a therapeutic and transformative way.

E. Hypnosis

Hypnosis is a state of focused attention and relaxation that allows access to the subconscious mind. Individuals may recall past events and memories that were previously beyond their conscious reach while under hypnosis.

V. Moral and Ethical Considerations

Understanding and influencing behaviour via the subconscious mind raises significant ethical and moral issues. Exploration and modification of subconscious beliefs and behaviour must be approached with sensitivity and respect for individual autonomy and cultural differences. Individuals and therapists must be aware of potential ethical issues and ensure that the process is carried out responsibly and ethically.

VI. Conclusion

The influence of the subconscious mind on behaviour is an enthralling aspect of human psychology. It influences our habits, emotional responses, decision-making, and creative thinking, often without our knowledge. Individuals can take steps towards personal growth, self-improvement, and a more intentional and fulfilling life by gaining a deeper understanding of the subconscious mind and employing various techniques to access and influence its processes. When the subconscious mind is harnessed and aligned with conscious goals and values, it can lead to transformative changes in behaviour and overall well-being.

5. Problem Solving in the Subconscious Mind:

Problem solving is a fundamental cognitive process that assists people in navigating life's challenges and complexities. While conscious problem solving is a well-studied and recognised aspect of human cognition, the subconscious mind plays an important role in this domain as well. We will delve into the intricate workings of problem solving in the subconscious mind, its mechanisms, and how it influences our thoughts, creativity, and decision-making in this comprehensive exploration.

I. The Subconscious Mind:

The subconscious mind is a psychological concept that refers to the part of the mind that operates below the level of conscious awareness. It stores a wide range of information, experiences, emotions, and beliefs that influence human cognition and behaviour.

A. Problem Solving Methods: Conscious vs. Subconscious

Problem solving is not limited to deliberate, conscious thought processes. The subconscious mind solves problems as well, often without our conscious awareness. While conscious problem solving involves deliberate analysis and reasoning, subconscious problem solving occurs in the background, generating insights and solutions that appear "out of nowhere."

B. The role in Day-to-Day Problem Solving

The subconscious mind plays an essential role in everyday problem solving. While we go about our daily lives, it works on challenges and issues, providing solutions, making connections, and generating creative ideas. It can be especially useful when dealing with complex or emotionally charged issues

II. Problem Solving Mechanisms in the Subconscious Mind

To comprehend how the subconscious mind engages in problem solving, it is critical to investigate some key mechanisms and processes:

A. Processing of Information

The subconscious mind is an extremely capable information processor. Even without conscious awareness, it can manage massive amounts of data and sensory input. This information processing enables it to analyse problems, consider various factors, and connect seemingly unrelated bits of information.

B. Memory Retrieval

When attempting to solve a problem, the subconscious mind consults stored memories and experiences. It searches this vast database for relevant information, analogies, and patterns that can be applied to the current issue.

C. Recognition of Patterns

The subconscious mind's primary function is to recognise patterns. It is particularly good at detecting similarities and differences between various stimuli, experiences, and situations. This ability enables it to identify patterns and relationships that can be used to solve problems.

D. Emotionally Motivated Problem Solving

In the subconscious mind, emotions are inextricably linked to problem solving. Emotions can give a problem a sense of urgency or importance, causing the subconscious to seek solutions. In life-threatening situations, for example, the emotional motivation to protect loved ones can lead to creative problem solving.

E. Subconscious Processing

The subconscious mind frequently works on issues in the background. When confronted with a problem, it continues to think about it even when the conscious mind is preoccupied with other things. This subconscious processing can result in "aha!" moments when solutions suddenly become conscious.

III. Creativity and Problem Solving

Creativity and problem solving are inextricably linked, and the subconscious mind plays a vital role in encouraging creative solutions to complex problems.

A. Unconscious Incubation

The subconscious mind engages in an unconscious incubation process, which allows problems to percolate and evolve without conscious intervention. The mind explores various possibilities, makes connections, and generates creative ideas that can lead to innovative solutions during this incubation period.

B. Associative Thinking

In the subconscious mind, associative thinking is an important component of creativity and problem solving. It makes connections and analogies by drawing on the vast pool of information and experiences stored in the subconscious. These connections can lead to new approaches to old problems.

C. Daydreaming and Mind Wandering

Daydreaming and mind wandering are manifestations of the subconscious mind at work. The mind is free to explore unstructured thinking, make associations, and consider unconventional ideas during these states. These mental processes have the potential to pave the way for creative problem solving.

D. Dreams

Dreams are a strong manifestation of the subconscious mind's problem-solving abilities. Dreams can provide new perspectives, creative solutions, and insights into unresolved issues. Dreams that provided innovative solutions inspired many famous inventions and artistic creations.

IV. Subconscious Problem Solving in Creative Fields

The problem-solving abilities of the subconscious mind are especially prominent in creative fields such as art, music, literature, and science.

A. Art and Music

Artists and musicians frequently rely on their subconscious minds for creative ideas and solutions. The subconscious can help with music composition, artwork creation, and the development of new artistic styles.

B. Literature and Writing

The power of the subconscious mind in problem solving is frequently experienced by writers. It can aid in the resolution of writer's block, the development of plotlines, and the selection of appropriate words and phrases. The "flow" state that writers experience is frequently the result of subconscious problem solving.

C. Scientific Discoveries

Scientists and researchers have reported insights and discoveries that appear to come from the subconscious mind. Subconscious processing has the potential to lead to scientific breakthroughs and novel approaches to complex research problems.

V. Accessing the Subconscious Mind to Solve Problems

While the subconscious mind automatically solves problems, individuals can take deliberate steps to access and harness its creative problem-solving abilities:

A. Relaxation and Mindfulness

Relaxation and mindfulness practises can help to quiet the conscious mind and make room for the subconscious. Individuals create a conducive environment for subconscious problem solving by reducing stress and mental clutter.

B. Sleep and Dream Analysis

Sleep is important for subconscious problem solving. Keeping a dream journal and analysing dreams can provide insights and novel solutions to unresolved issues. Dreams frequently reveal hidden connections and opportunities.

C. Expression of Creativity

Participating in creative activities such as art, writing, or music can help to unlock the subconscious mind's problem-solving potential. The act of creation promotes associative thinking and innovative problem solving.

D. Mindfulness

Meditation is a technique that can help you gain access to your subconscious mind. Individuals may experience moments of insight and creative problem solving simply by paying attention and quieting conscious thought.

E. Problem Solving Through Storytelling

Narrative therapy and storytelling techniques encourage people to explore problems through the use of narratives and metaphors. Through storytelling, these approaches tap into the subconscious mind's ability to generate creative solutions.

VI. Ethical Considerations

Understanding and influencing subconscious problem solving raises ethical concerns, especially in the creative and scientific fields. In problem solving that involves the subconscious mind, it is critical to maintain a sense of responsibility, authenticity, and integrity. Even if innovative solutions emerge from the subconscious, proper credit and acknowledgment should be given to the source.

Conclusion VII.

Problem solving in the subconscious mind is an enthralling aspect of human cognition that is required for creativity, innovation, and everyday decision-making. Beyond conscious awareness, the subconscious mind processes information, makes connections, and generates creative solutions to complex problems. Individuals can tap into a wellspring of creative thinking and gain fresh perspectives on challenges by recognising the value of the subconscious mind in problem solving and adopting strategies to access its potential. The subconscious mind's problem-solving abilities, whether in art, science, or daily life, provide a wealth of innovative solutions and insights that enrich our understanding of the world and our ability to navigate it.

6. Visualisation and Affirmation in the Subconscious Mind (Unlocking the Potential of Positive Change):

Visualisation and affirmation are powerful techniques that tap into the subconscious mind's potential to bring about positive change and personal transformation. These techniques make use of the mind's ability to influence thoughts, emotions, and behaviours, thereby shaping the reality we experience. We will delve into the intricate workings of visualisation and affirmation in the subconscious mind, their mechanisms, and how they can be used to achieve personal goals and aspirations in this comprehensive exploration.

I. An Overview of the Subconscious Mind

Throughout the history of psychology, the concept of the subconscious mind has been a source of fascination and investigation. It is a vast and intricate realm within our psyche that operates beneath the surface of conscious awareness and influences various aspects of human cognition and behaviour.

A. The Importance of Belief Systems

Belief systems, which are embedded in the subconscious mind, have a significant influence on our perceptions and behaviours. These beliefs, formed through a combination of experiences, cultural influences, and personal values, are powerful forces that shape the course of our lives.

B. Emotional Influence

Emotions weave intricately through the subconscious realm. These emotions, which are triggered by hidden thoughts, beliefs, and memories, have a significant influence on our actions. Unleashing the power of emotions is a critical component of using visualisation and affirmation to foster positive transformations.

II. Visualisation: The Power of Mental Imagery

Visualisation is a technique in which vivid mental images of desired outcomes or experiences are created. This technique uses the subconscious mind's ability to respond to mental imagery, influencing thoughts, emotions, and behaviours.

A. Mechanisms of Visualisation

- Mental Rehearsal: Visualisation is a type of mental rehearsal in which people mentally simulate different scenarios or events. This practise allows the subconscious mind to become acquainted with the desired outcome.

- Activation of the Reticular Activating System (RAS): The RAS is a part of the brain that filters information and prioritises what enters conscious awareness. Visualisation can assist in directing the RAS's attention to elements related to the desired goal or experience.

• Emotional Engagement: Visualisation frequently elicits strong emotions, which are important in activating the subconscious mind. Emotional involvement heightens the impact of mental imagery.

B. Positive Change Through Visualisation

Personal development, goal achievement, and problem solving can all benefit from visualisation. Individuals can create a powerful connection between their subconscious beliefs and their conscious efforts by visualising a desired outcome or goal on a regular basis.

• Goal Achievement: Visualising the successful accomplishment of goals, whether personal, professional, or health-related, can reinforce the subconscious commitment to the desired outcome.

• Stress Reduction: By creating a mental refuge or calming scenario that the subconscious mind can access when needed, visualisation can help reduce stress and anxiety.

• Improved Performance: Athletes, artists, and people from all walks of life use visualisation to improve their performance. They prime their subconscious for success by mentally rehearsing their actions and outcomes.

III. Affirmation: The Power of Positive Self-Talk

Affirmations are short, positive statements that are repeated in order to reinforce a desired belief or behaviour. Affirmations work by gradually reshaping beliefs and attitudes by influencing the subconscious mind.

A. Mechanisms of Affirmation

• Repetition: Consistent repetition of affirmations is essential for programming the subconscious mind. This repetition helps to deeply embed the desired belief or behaviour within the subconscious.

• Cognitive Dissonance: When affirmations contradict existing negative beliefs, they can cause a state of cognitive dissonance. Because of the discomfort, the subconscious mind adapts by aligning with the positive affirmation.

• Self-reflective thoughts: Affirmations improve self-concept and self-esteem by encouraging positive self-talk.

B. Positive Change Through Affirmation

Affirmations can be used in a variety of situations to promote personal growth and development.

• Self-Confidence: By challenging self-doubt and reinforcing a positive self-image, affirmations can help boost self-confidence. Affirmations such as "I am confident and capable" can help to build confidence over time.

• Health and Wellness: Affirmations can be used to encourage healthy behaviours and lifestyle modifications. Affirmations such as "I am committed to making healthy choices" can help to reinforce positive habits.

• Stress Management: Affirmations can help to reduce stress by instilling a sense of calm and resilience. Statements such as "I am at peace with the present moment" can help in stress management.

IV. The Power of Visualisation and Affirmation

Affirmation and visualisation combined can be a powerful tool for personal transformation. These practises work together to engage the subconscious mind and effect long-term, positive change.

A. Visualisation and Affirmation for Goal Achievement

When used in tandem, visualisation and affirmation assist individuals in setting clear goals, creating a compelling mental image of their desired outcomes, and reinforcing these goals with positive self-talk. This combination is especially effective at achieving personal and professional goals.

B. Emotional Involvement

Both visualisation and affirmation have an emotional component that is critical to their effectiveness. When emotions are involved, the subconscious mind is more likely to respond and integrate the desired beliefs and behaviours.

C. Developing Resilience

Visualisation and affirmation can help people build emotional resilience by helping them deal with setbacks and challenges in a positive way. These practises can help individuals overcome obstacles and maintain a positive outlook by priming the subconscious mind.

V. Practical Application of Visualisation and Affirmation

There are several key steps to using visualisation and affirmation for personal development and positive change:

• Goal Setting: Define your goals and aspirations clearly, making sure they are specific, measurable, achievable, relevant, and time-bound (SMART goals).

• Create Visualisations: Create detailed mental images of yourself successfully achieving your goals or experiencing the desired outcomes. Use all of your senses to make the visualisations as vivid and realistic as possible.

• Create Affirmations: Create affirmations that support your desired goals and beliefs. Positive, present-tense, and personal affirmations should be used.

• Repetition: Repeat your affirmations and engage in daily visualisation sessions on a regular basis. Repetition is necessary to ensure that the message is deeply ingrained in the subconscious mind.

• Emotion and Belief: As you engage in visualisation and affirmation, pay attention to the emotions you associate with reaching your goals. Belief in the process is essential for its success.

• Patience and Persistence: Recognise that changing beliefs and behaviours takes time. Be patient and persistent in your practise, and believe in your subconscious mind's ability to effect positive change.

VI. Ethical Considerations

While visualisation and affirmation are powerful tools for personal development, it is essential to approach them ethically:

• Honesty and Realism: Make certain that the goals and affirmations you set are honest, realistic, and in line with your values. For genuine personal growth, you must be honest with yourself.

• Responsibility: Recognise that personal change necessitates effort, action, and responsibility on your part. Visualisation and affirmation are not intended to replace action, but rather to supplement and guide it.

• Ethical Alignment: Ensure that the goals and changes you seek are consistent with ethical principles and take into account the impact on others and the broader community.

VII. Conclusion

Visualisation and affirmation are powerful techniques for releasing the subconscious mind's power to effect positive change and personal transformation. Individuals can actively shape their reality and achieve their goals and aspirations by harnessing the subconscious mind's ability to influence thoughts, emotions, and behaviours. Visualisation and affirmation work together to engage the subconscious, encourage emotional engagement, and build resilience in the face of adversity. While patience and persistence are required, these practises provide a path to personal growth, self-improvement, and a more fulfilling life. You can embark on a journey of self-discovery and positive change by embracing the potential of your subconscious mind, realising your full potential and experiencing the transformative power of visualisation and affirmation.

7. The Science and Application of Hypnosis in the Subconscious Mind

Hypnosis is a fascinating psychological phenomenon that taps into the subconscious mind's power. Hypnosis, which is frequently portrayed in popular culture as a mysterious trance-like state, is a well-documented and scientifically studied process with real-world applications ranging from therapy to personal development. We will delve into the science of hypnosis, how it interacts with the subconscious mind, and its practical applications for healing, personal growth, and behaviour modification in this comprehensive exploration.

I. What Exactly Is Hypnosis?

Hypnosis is a trance-like state characterised by focused attention and increased suggestibility. Individuals in this state are more open to suggestions and may experience changes in perception, memory, and behaviour. It is frequently accomplished with the assistance of a trained therapist or through self-hypnosis techniques.

A. Historical Overview

Hypnosis has been practised since ancient civilizations. However, it wasn't until the late 18th century that a physician named Franz Mesmer became famous for his "mesmerism" techniques, which laid the groundwork for modern hypnosis. In the 19th century, Scottish surgeon James Braid coined the term "hypnosis," which is derived from the Greek word "hypnos," which means sleep. He recognised that the hypnotic state was distinct from sleep and was associated with increased suggestibility.

B. The Science of Hypnosis

While once shrouded in mystery and mysticism, hypnosis is now recognised as a legitimate psychological phenomenon with a growing body of empirical research. Changes in brain activity occur during hypnosis, particularly in areas related to attention and suggestibility. Neuroimaging studies have revealed that the brain changes during hypnosis, implying that it is not merely a theatrical act but a genuine mental state.

II. The Subconscious Mind and Hypnosis

The subconscious mind is closely linked to hypnosis. The altered state of consciousness that hypnosis induces allows for greater access to and control over subconscious processes.

A. The Role of Suggestion

Suggestion is a key component of hypnosis. Individuals in a hypnotic state are more open to suggestions from the hypnotist. By directly addressing the subconscious mind, these suggestions can influence perceptions, beliefs, and behaviours.

B. Subconscious Processing

During hypnosis, the subconscious mind processes suggestions in a unique way. While the conscious mind may resist certain ideas or instructions, the subconscious is more receptive, which is why hypnosis is frequently used to modify subconscious behaviours or beliefs.

C. Overcoming Inhibitions

Individuals can use hypnosis to overcome inhibitions and reservations that are often rooted in the subconscious mind. People may be more willing to explore and address personal issues and deeply held beliefs that influence their actions when they are in this state.

III. Applications of Hypnosis

Hypnosis has numerous applications, many of which leverage of its influence on the subconscious mind.

A. Hypnotherapy

Hypnotherapy is the therapeutic application of hypnosis. It is used to treat a wide range of problems, including anxiety, phobias, smoking cessation, weight loss, and pain management. Hypnotherapy can help people discover and change subconscious beliefs and behaviours that are contributing to their problems.

B. Behavioural Modification

By focusing on the subconscious mind, hypnosis can be used to change unwanted behaviours or habits. This includes issues such as binge eating, nail-biting, and substance abuse. Healthy patterns and attitudes can be influenced by the subconscious.

C. Pain Management

Hypnosis has been used to manage and alleviate acute and chronic pain. Individuals can learn to change their perception of pain and develop better coping strategies by tapping into their subconscious mind.

D. Stress Reduction

Relaxation and stress reduction can be achieved through hypnosis. Techniques such as progressive muscle relaxation and guided imagery help people achieve a deep state of relaxation, which improves their overall well-being and reduces stress.

E. Memory Improvement

Memory enhancement and recall can be aided by hypnosis. It can be used to recover repressed memories or to improve memory function, allowing people to access information stored in their subconscious minds.

F. Creative Exploration

Hypnosis has been used as a creative exploration tool. Individuals may access their subconscious during a trance-like state to stimulate creative thinking, problem-solving, and artistic inspiration.

IV. The Process of Hypnosis

Several key stages are usually involved in hypnosis:

A. Induction

The individual is guided into a state of heightened suggestibility during the induction phase. Relaxation techniques, guided imagery, and focused attention are used to accomplish this.

B. Deepening

There is usually a deepening phase following induction. The goal is to deepen the hypnotic state and increase the person's receptivity to suggestions. Progressive relaxation or imagery may be used to deepen the experience.

C. Suggestion

During this stage, the hypnotist provides suggestions based on the individual's goals or therapeutic needs. These suggestions may be directed at specific issues or behaviours, encouraging the subconscious mind to respond positively.

D. Post-Hypnotic Suggestions

Post-hypnotic suggestions are instructions given during a hypnotic state that are intended to influence the individual after the session is over. These can be used as "homework" to help reinforce the desired changes.

E. Termination

The hypnotist usually ends the session, bringing the individual out of the hypnotic state and back to their normal level of consciousness.

V. Self-Hypnosis

Self-hypnosis is a valuable skill that people can use to improve themselves and grow personally. It entails self-inducing hypnosis and delivering suggestions or affirmations to the subconscious mind.

A. Learning Self-Hypnosis

Learning self-hypnosis frequently entails mastering relaxation techniques, visualisation, and the ability to concentrate. Self-hypnosis skills can be developed using a variety of resources, including books and guided recordings.

B. Self-Hypnosis for Personal Development

Self-hypnosis can be used to achieve a variety of personal development goals, including increasing self-confidence and overcoming anxiety. Individuals can directly influence their subconscious mind to facilitate positive change by using self-hypnosis.

VI. Ethical Considerations

While hypnosis can be an effective tool for personal development and therapy, it raises serious ethical concerns. These are a few examples:

A. Affirmative Consent

Hypnosis should always be used with the individual's informed consent. They must be aware of the process and its purpose, as well as any potential risks.

B. The Hypnotist's Role

Hypnotists should be well-trained, ethical professionals who use their abilities responsibly and to the benefit of their clients. They must respect personal boundaries and never use hypnosis for unethical purposes.

C. Recall of Memories

Hypnosis can help with memory recall, but it should be used with caution because it can be unreliable. Given the possibility of false memories, recovered memories should be handled with caution.

D. Responsibility

Individuals who use self-hypnosis or undergo hypnotherapy are responsible for their own well-being and decisions. Although hypnosis is a useful tool for personal development, the individual is ultimately responsible for their own decisions and actions.

VII. Conclusion

Hypnosis is a fascinating psychological phenomenon that uses the subconscious mind's power to effect change and personal growth. Individuals can gain access to a valuable tool for addressing issues, changing behaviours, and improving their overall well-being by understanding the science of hypnosis and its interaction with the subconscious. The subconscious mind can be used to support positive transformations and empower individuals to achieve their goals and aspirations, whether through hypnotherapy or self-hypnosis. Hypnosis can be a valuable and effective method for unlocking the potential of the subconscious mind in the right hands and with ethical considerations in mind.

8. The Placebo Effect in the Subconscious Mind (Unravel the Secrets of Belief):

The placebo effect is a remarkable and well-documented phenomenon in medical and psychological fields that demonstrates the subconscious mind's profound influence on human health and well-being. It happens when people experience real improvements in their condition or symptoms solely because they believe they are receiving a beneficial treatment, even if the treatment itself is inactive or inert. In this comprehensive investigation, we will delve into the science and mechanisms of the placebo effect, its impact on health and healing, and the role of the subconscious mind in producing these outstanding outcomes.

I. An Overview of the Placebo Effect

The placebo effect demonstrates the complex interplay between the mind and body. It is frequently observed in clinical trials, where participants receiving an inactive substance, such as a sugar pill or saline solution, report improved health. These improvements are not due to the placebo's physical properties, but rather to the individual's belief in the treatment's efficacy.

A. Historical Overview

The word "placebo" comes from the Latin for "I shall please." Historically, physicians used placebos to pacify patients and were thought to be deceptive. However, the placebo effect gained recognition over time and has since been extensively studied.

B. The Nocebo Effect

Individuals experiencing negative effects due to their belief that a treatment will harm them, even if the treatment itself is inert, are said to be experiencing the "nocebo" effect. The nocebo effect emphasises the subconscious mind's powerful role in influencing perceptions of health and well-being.

II. The Mechanisms of the Placebo Effect

The placebo effect works via a number of intricate mechanisms, many of which are deeply ingrained in the subconscious mind.

A. Expectation and Belief

The placebo effect is heavily reliant on expectation and belief. When people believe they are receiving a treatment that will help them, their minds react by releasing natural chemicals and neurotransmitters that promote healing. These beliefs stimulate the brain's reward centres, causing endorphins and other beneficial substances to be released.

B. The Brain-Body Connection

The release of neurotransmitters, hormones, and other signalling molecules by the brain allows it to communicate with the rest of the body. Belief in a treatment's efficacy can cause the brain to release substances that modulate pain, inflammation, and other physiological processes. This demonstrates the mind's and body's profound interconnectedness.

C. Neurotransmitters and Hormones

The placebo effect has been linked to the release of neurotransmitters such as endorphins, dopamine, and serotonin, all of which are known to improve mood, reduce pain, and boost well-being. Furthermore, belief in a treatment can alter hormone levels, affecting stress responses and immune function.

III. Medical Placebo Effects

The placebo effect has been observed in a variety of medical and clinical settings, affecting a wide range of conditions and treatments.

A. Pain Relief

Placebos can effectively reduce pain perception. Individuals' pain thresholds may rise when they believe they are receiving an analgesic treatment, and they may report feeling less pain. This phenomenon has been observed in a number of pain-related conditions, ranging from headaches to chronic pain.

B. Mood and Mental Health

The placebo effect has the potential to influence mood and mental health conditions. Individuals who believed they were receiving active treatment in studies of depression and anxiety reported improvements in their symptoms, even when the treatment was inert.

C. Digestive Issues

When patients with conditions such as irritable bowel syndrome (IBS) believed they were receiving a beneficial treatment, their symptoms improved. The placebo effect has been observed in gastrointestinal disorders, implying that it can have an effect on gut function.

D. Immune Responses

Belief in a treatment can have an impact on immune responses. Participants receiving placebos in clinical trials demonstrated increased immune activity, such as antibody production, comparable to those receiving active treatments. This suggests that the placebo effect has the potential to stimulate the immune system.

E. Parkinson's disease

The placebo effect has been observed even in Parkinson's disease, where neurotransmitter imbalances are prominent. Patients who believed they were receiving treatment for their condition had improved motor functions, demonstrating the importance of belief in influencing neurochemistry.

IV. The Role of the Subconscious Mind

The subconscious mind is a central player in the placebo effect, as it houses our beliefs, expectations, and the neural networks that respond to suggestion.

A. Conditioning and Suggestion

Conditioning and suggestion have a strong influence on the subconscious mind. When people repeatedly see positive results from a particular treatment, they become conditioned to believe in its efficacy. This conditioning can create a subconscious expectation of improvement, triggering the placebo effect.

B. Psychological Factors

The placebo effect is also influenced by psychological factors such as hope, optimism, and the doctor-patient relationship. Positive interactions with healthcare providers and a patient's trust in their treatment can increase belief in the efficacy of the treatment, reinforcing the placebo effect.

C. The Strength of Belief

The placebo effect is founded on belief. Based on what a person believes to be true, the subconscious mind can generate physical responses. This emphasises the importance of the subconscious in shaping a person's perception of health and healing.

V. Ethical Considerations

In medical and clinical practise, the placebo effect poses ethical challenges. While placebos can produce real health benefits, their use as deceptive treatments raises concerns about informed consent and honesty in patient care.

A. Affirmative Consent

Informed consent is a fundamental ethical principle in medical practise. Patients have the right to be informed about the nature of their treatment, as well as the potential risks and benefits. This principle may be violated if placebos are used without the patients' knowledge.

B. Ethical Quandary

When considering how to harness the benefits of the placebo effect while maintaining transparency and patient autonomy, an ethical quandary arises. Open-label placebos (in which patients are aware they are receiving inert treatments) or using placebos as adjunct therapies in addition to standard care are examples of ethical approaches.

VI. Conclusion

The placebo effect is an intriguing phenomenon that highlights the significant role of the subconscious mind in health and healing. It has been observed in a variety of medical conditions and treatments, highlighting the mind-body connection. While the placebo effect raises ethical concerns in clinical practise, it also provides an opportunity to investigate the mind's extraordinary ability to influence health and well-being. Understanding the mechanisms of the placebo effect and its reliance on belief and expectation allows healthcare providers to use this mind-body connection for the benefit of patients in an ethical and transparent manner. The placebo effect begs further investigation into the complex relationship between the conscious and subconscious mind, as well as its impact on human health and healing.

9. Overcoming Limiting Beliefs in the Subconscious Mind (Breaking Free):

Limiting beliefs are deeply ingrained thought patterns and convictions that limit a person's potential, impede personal growth, and undermine self-confidence. These beliefs are frequently formed subconsciously and can be rooted in previous experiences, cultural conditioning, or self-perception. This in-depth investigation delves into the nature of limiting beliefs, their origins, impact, and strategies for identifying and overcoming them, ultimately unlocking the subconscious mind's full potential.

I. An Overview of Limiting Beliefs

Limiting beliefs are self-imposed impediments that keep people from reaching their full potential. These beliefs are frequently found in the subconscious mind, where they influence thoughts, emotions, and behaviours. Examples include thoughts such as "I'm not good enough," "I'll never succeed," and "I don't deserve happiness."

A. The Roots of Limiting Beliefs

Limiting beliefs can arise from a variety of sources, including:

1. Childhood Experiences: Early experiences, especially those involving criticism, rejection, or failure, can shape negative beliefs about one's own worth and abilities.

2. Cultural and Societal influences: Cultural norms, societal expectations, and stereotypes can all reinforce limiting beliefs about one's identity and role in society.

3. Fear of Failure: Failures or setbacks in the past can lead to beliefs that limit one's willingness to take risks or pursue new opportunities in the future.

4. Negative Self-Perception: How people see themselves, their strengths and weaknesses, can lead to limiting beliefs that lower self-esteem.

B. The Effects of Limiting Beliefs

Limiting beliefs have an enormous effect on a person's life and well-being:

1. Self-Sabotage: Believing in one's own limitations can lead to self-sabotage, causing people to avoid challenges, procrastinate, or accept mediocrity.

2. Anxiety and Stress: Limiting beliefs can increase anxiety and stress because people are concerned about not meeting their own or others' expectations.

3. Reduced Self-Confidence: These beliefs erode self-confidence and impair a person's ability to take on new challenges or pursue their goals.

4. Reduced Resilience: Limiting beliefs can impair resilience, making it difficult to recover from setbacks and challenges.

II. Recognising Limiting Beliefs

Recognising and identifying limiting beliefs are vital steps in breaking free from them. Because these beliefs are frequently found in the subconscious mind, they may not be immediately apparent.

A. Self-Reflection

Self-reflection is an effective tool for identifying limiting beliefs. It entails investigating one's thoughts, emotions, and self-perception. Self-reflection can be aided by journaling, meditation, and mindfulness practises.

B. Pattern Recognition

Behaviour patterns, particularly those involving avoidance, procrastination, or negative self-talk, can indicate the presence of limiting beliefs. Recognising recurring patterns can reveal information about underlying beliefs.

C. Obtaining Feedback

Reaching out to trusted friends, family members, or a therapist can provide valuable insights into the beliefs that are potentially holding you back. They can provide a different perspective and aid in the identification of thought patterns.

D. Examining Trigger Events

The presence of limiting beliefs can be revealed by recalling specific situations or experiences that elicit strong negative emotions. Examining one's thoughts and emotions in relation to these events can provide insights.

III. Overcoming Limiting Beliefs

Overcoming limiting beliefs is a transformative process that requires conscious effort and compassion for oneself. It necessitates strategies to challenge these beliefs and replace them with more empowering ones.

A. Cognitive Restructuring

Identifying and challenging negative thought patterns is part of cognitive restructuring. Individuals can use this process to reframe their beliefs and replace them with more constructive ones. Among the techniques are:

1. Self-examination: Examining the evidence that supports or contradicts limiting beliefs.

2. Positive affirmations: Emphasising positive and empowering things to yourself to counteract negative self-talk.

3. Visualisation: To reinforce empowering beliefs, create vivid mental images of success and positive outcomes.

B. Compassion for Oneself

Self-compassion is essential in the process of overcoming limiting beliefs. Self-acceptance and resilience can be fostered by treating oneself with kindness and understanding rather than self-criticism.

C. Establishing Realistic Goals

Setting attainable goals and breaking them down into smaller, manageable steps can help to boost self-esteem and gradually challenge limiting beliefs.

D. Seeking Support

Therapists, counsellors, and support groups can offer guidance and a safe environment in which to explore and address limiting beliefs. They provide tools and strategies to encourage personal development and self-empowerment.

E. Developing a Growth Mindset

Adopting a growth mindset entails viewing setbacks and challenges as opportunities for learning and growth. This shift in perspective fosters resilience and faith in one's own ability to improve.

IV. The Function of the Subconscious Mind

The subconscious mind shapes limiting beliefs and is thus an important component in their resolution.

A. Subconscious Programming

Many limiting beliefs are the result of subconscious programming, which is often ingrained in children. Because these beliefs are deeply embedded in the subconscious mind, they can persist.

B. Subconscious Reprogramming

Reprogramming the subconscious mind entails making conscious efforts to replace limiting beliefs with empowering beliefs. Visualisation, hypnotherapy, and mindfulness practises are examples of techniques that engage the subconscious in the process of change.

C. Conscious and Subconscious Mind Alignment

Overcoming limiting beliefs requires achieving harmony between the conscious and subconscious minds. Goals can be set by the conscious mind, but the subconscious mind provides the underlying beliefs and motivation to pursue them.

V. Success Stories

Many people have successfully overcome limiting beliefs in order to achieve their goals and reach their full potential. These personal transformation stories demonstrate the power of self-awareness, determination, and the ability to challenge deeply held beliefs.

A. Oprah Winfrey

After overcoming a difficult childhood and self-doubt, Oprah rose to prominence as a media mogul, talk show host, and philanthropist. Her success can be attributed to challenging her limiting beliefs and embracing personal growth.

B. J. K. Rowling

Before becoming a literary success, the author of the Harry Potter series faced numerous rejections. Her faith in her story and ability to persevere in the face of adversity demonstrate the power of perseverance.

C. Thomas Edison

Edison, who held over a thousand patents, famously stated, "I have not failed. I've just found 10,000 ways that won't work." His tenacity and belief in his innovations demonstrate his capacity for growth and success.

VI. Ethical Considerations

Overcoming limiting beliefs raises ethical concerns, especially when dealing with deeply ingrained beliefs influenced by trauma or societal conditioning. This process must be approached with sensitivity and respect for each individual's unique experiences and challenges.

A. Respecting Autonomy

Individuals should have the freedom to choose when and how to address their limiting beliefs. It is unethical to press or coerce someone to confront these beliefs.

B. Trauma-Informed Care

Trauma-informed care and therapy are essential when limiting beliefs are rooted in traumatic experiences. In their journey towards healing and self-empowerment, trauma survivors require specialised support and understanding.

VII. Conclusion

Limiting beliefs can stifle personal growth, undermine self-confidence, and impede success because they are deeply embedded in the subconscious mind. Recognising these beliefs, understanding their origins, and implementing strategies to challenge and replace them are all necessary steps in unlocking the subconscious mind's full potential. Individuals can overcome limiting beliefs and embark on a transformative journey of self-discovery and empowerment by using cognitive restructuring, self-compassion, and a growth mindset. The subconscious mind's role in shaping and reshaping beliefs emphasises the profound connection between the conscious and subconscious aspects of the self, providing the opportunity for profound personal growth and liberation from self-imposed limitations.

The subconscious mind has negative impacts which can lead to negative outcomes when certain aspects or beliefs do not align with our conscious goals and desires. Here are some examples of how the subconscious mind can have a negative impact on our daily lives:

1. Negative Self-Talk: Negative self-talk generated by the subconscious mind can erode self-worth and create a pessimistic outlook. Constant negative self-talk can cause anxiety, stress, and depression, negatively impacting overall mental health.

2. Procrastination and Resistance: The subconscious mind may resist change or avoid discomfort, resulting in procrastination and resistance of difficult or necessary tasks. This can stifle personal and professional development.

3. Emotional Reactions: Negative emotions and past traumas stored in the subconscious mind can influence current emotional reactions. Unresolved emotional issues can cause mood swings, rage, or anxiety, which can interfere with daily interactions and well-being.

4. Limiting Beliefs: The subconscious mind can harbour limiting beliefs, which are frequently formed in childhood or through previous experiences. These beliefs can lead to self-doubt, low self-esteem, and insecurity. Believing, for example, that "I'm not good enough" can stifle personal growth and success.

5. Self-Sabotage: Self-sabotage can be caused by subconscious beliefs and fears. For example, fear of failure may prevent a person from pursuing opportunities, limiting personal and professional development.

6. Addictive Behaviour: Since it stores memories of pleasurable experiences associated with substances or activities, the subconscious mind can drive addictive behaviour. This can result in bad habits and addiction.

7. Limiting Mindsets: Fixed mindsets, which are characterised by the belief that abilities and intelligence are static, can have subconscious roots. People with this mindset may avoid challenges or efforts to learn and grow, which can stifle personal development.

8. Resistance to Change: Even if the change is positive or necessary for growth, the subconscious mind often resists it. This resistance can take the form of anxiety, fear, or a reluctance to leave one's comfort zone.

9. Stress and Anxiety: Unresolved fears and anxieties stored in the subconscious can lead to chronic stress and anxiety disorders. These conditions can have a major negative impact on daily life, affecting both physical and mental health.

10. Interpersonal Conflicts: The subconscious memories and emotional responses can lead to misunderstandings, conflicts, or relationship problems with family, friends, and colleagues.

11. Unhealthy Coping Mechanisms: Coping mechanisms stored in the subconscious mind, such as emotional eating, substance abuse, or avoidance, can be unhealthy. These behaviours can be harmful to one's health and overall well-being.

12. Self-Fulfilling Prophecies: Negative beliefs in the subconscious can lead to self-fulfilling prophecies. For example, if a person believes they are doomed to fail, they may not put forth the necessary effort to succeed, thereby confirming their belief.

Recognising and dealing with the negative impact of the subconscious mind requires self-awareness, mindfulness, and deliberate practises to reprogram limiting beliefs and emotions. Cognitive restructuring, positive affirmations, therapy and self-reflection are all techniques that can help people align their conscious goals with their subconscious beliefs, resulting in personal growth, improved well-being, and a more fulfilling daily life.

While the subconscious mind can have negative consequences, it can also have a significant positive impact on our daily lives, contributing to our happiness, personal growth, and overall success. Here are some examples of how the subconscious mind can positively influence our daily lives:

1. Habitual Behaviours: The subconscious mind assists in the automation of daily routines and habits. This can be advantageous when it comes to healthy habits such as exercise, proper nutrition, and adequate rest. Positive behaviours that become habitual require less conscious effort to maintain, making it easier to live a healthy lifestyle.

2. Intuition and Decision-Making: Intuition, which is frequently attributed to the subconscious mind, can provide useful insights and guide decision-making. Trusting your instincts can lead to better decisions in a variety of life situations, from personal relationships to problem-solving at work.

3. Memory and Learning: The subconscious mind is important for memory and learning. It stores massive amounts of data, allowing us to recall important facts, past experiences, and learned skills. This knowledge is priceless for personal and professional development.

4. Creativity and Problem Solving: The subconscious mind is a creative wellspring. When we are not consciously focused on a task, the subconscious generates many innovative ideas and problem-solving solutions. This can result in breakthroughs in creative endeavours and professional challenges.

5. Emotional Regulation: The subconscious mind can aid in the regulation of emotions and the management of stress. Mindfulness, meditation, and deep breathing techniques all engage the subconscious, resulting in improved emotional well-being and stress reduction.

6. Self-Image and Confidence: The subconscious mind fosters positive self-beliefs and self-confidence. Individuals who have a positive self-image and believe in their abilities are more likely to achieve their goals and succeed in various aspects of life.

7. Goal Achievement: Visualisation and positive affirmations can help the subconscious mind support goal achievement. Those engage their subconscious in working towards specific goals by repeatedly visualising their accomplishment.

8. Automatic Responses: Because of the subconscious mind, many daily responses and behaviours are automatic. This efficiency enables us to perform routine tasks like driving, typing or cooking with ease.

9. Emotional Resilience: The subconscious mind influences emotional resilience, or the ability to recover from setbacks and adversity. Positive beliefs and coping mechanisms stored in the subconscious mind can assist people in overcoming obstacles and maintaining mental and emotional well-being.

10. Emotional Intelligence: The subconscious mind plays an important part in emotional intelligence, which involves understanding, managing, and effectively using emotions. Relationships, communication, and interpersonal skills can all benefit from increased emotional intelligence.

11. Creativity and Inspiration: The subconscious mind can be a source of creative ideas and inspiration. Many artists, writers, and innovators attribute their breakthrough moments to the subconscious's creative potential.

12. Dreams and Problem Solving: Dreams often involve the subconscious mind resolving unresolved issues or challenges. Dream content can provide solutions to problems or fresh perspectives.

13. Personal Growth and Transformation: The subconscious mind can help with personal growth and transformation. Individuals can tap into the subconscious's capacity for change and development by challenging limiting beliefs and cultivating a growth mindset.

Understanding and harnessing the positive impacts of the subconscious mind requires deliberate practises such as visualisation, positive affirmations, mindfulness, and self-reflection. Individuals can unlock their full potential, promote well-being, and live more purposeful and fulfilling lives by aligning conscious goals and beliefs with the subconscious mind.

Certainly, here's a list of the negative and positive effects of the subconscious mind on daily life:

Aspect	Negative Impact	Positive Impact
Limiting Beliefs	Hinders self-confidence and personal growth.	Fosters self-confidence and goal achievement.
Negative Self-Talk	Undermines self-worth and generates pessimism.	Cultivates a positive outlook and self-esteem.
Procrastination and Resistance	Leads to avoidance and hinders progress.	Automates beneficial habits and routines.
Emotional Responses	Triggers mood swings and unresolved issues.	Supports emotional regulation and well-being.
Self-Sabotage	Prevents seizing opportunities and growth.	Encourages personal development and success.
Addictive Behavior	Drives unhealthy habits and addiction.	Stores learned skills and experiences.
Limiting Mindsets	Maintains a fixed mindset and avoidance.	Promotes a growth mindset and learning.
Resistance to	Creates fear and	Encourages

Change	reluctance to step outside comfort zone.	adaptability and personal growth.
Stress and Anxiety	Contributes to chronic stress and anxiety.	Supports stress management and emotional health.
Interpersonal Conflicts	Leads to misunderstandings and conflicts.	Enhances empathy and healthy relationships.
Unhealthy Coping Mechanisms	Promotes unhealthy coping mechanisms.	Fosters adaptive coping and resilience.
Self-Fulfilling Prophecies	Confirms negative beliefs through behavior.	Encourages positive behaviors and success.

Balancing and harnessing the subconscious mind's influence is essential for maximising positive and mitigating adverse impact in our daily lives. Self-awareness, mindfulness, and deliberate efforts to reprogram and align subconscious beliefs with conscious goals tend to be involved.

Psychology vs. Pseudosciences and Reverse Psychology

Psychology, palmistry, and physiognomy are three distinct fields that study human behaviour, personality, and character evaluation, albeit with varying degrees of scientific validity and acceptance. Here's a quick rundown of each:

1. Psychology:

• The scientific study of the mind and behaviour is known as psychology. It covers a broad range of topics, such as cognitive processes, emotional states, social interactions, and mental health. To understand and explain human behaviour, psychologists use empirical research and evidence-based methods.

• The scientific method is used in psychology to conduct experiments, collect data, and develop theories. It is regarded as a credible and evidence-based social science discipline.

• Psychologists diagnose and treat mental illnesses, provide counselling and therapy, conduct research on various aspects of human behaviour, and apply their knowledge in a variety of settings such as clinical, counselling, educational, and organisational psychology.

2. Palmistry:

• Palmistry, also known as chiromancy, is a method that entails reading the lines, forms, and markings on a person's hand's palm to reveal insights into their personality, future, and life path.

• Palmists believe that lines on the palm, such as the heart line, head line, and life line, can disclose information about a person's personality and future life events.

• Palmistry is not regarded as a scientifically valid or evidence-based technique, and it is frequently seen as a sort of divination or pseudoscience. Its accuracy and dependability are highly dubious.

3. Physiognomy:

• Physiognomy is the study of a person's facial features, particularly facial expressions and structures, to judge character, personality, and temperament.

• In the past, physiognomy involved analysing facial characteristics including the mouth, nose, and eyes. It was founded on the assumption that certain face traits might reflect inner qualities.

• Physiognomy is widely rejected as a valid approach of assessing personality in modern psychology and research. The concept that facial features may accurately predict a person's character or behaviour is not supported by scientific evidence.

Let's discuss each of these in more detail.

Psychology: A Comprehensive Examination of the Science of Mind and Behaviour

Psychology is a diverse and dynamic field of study that delves deeply into the complexities of human behaviour, cognition, and emotions. It aims to comprehend the mind's intricacies, the motivations behind our behaviours, and the influences that shape our thoughts and feelings. Psychology is a scientific field as well as an applied profession that plays an important role in our knowledge of human nature and in addressing a variety of real-world concerns.

At its foundation, psychology is the scientific study of the human mind and behaviour. It covers a wide range of topics and seeks fundamental answers to why humans think, feel, and act the way they do. It investigates the cognitive processes that underpin our thoughts and decisions, the emotions that impact our reactions, and the behaviours that manifest in different settings.

Psychology is a science that has both scientific and practical applications. It uses empirical research methods to collect data and build hypotheses that help us understand human behaviour. Furthermore, psychology has real-world applications ranging from clinical therapy to education and business, where psychological insights are used to solve problems and improve human well-being.

History

The history of psychology unfolds as an enthralling story, beginning with the ancient and pre-scientific period, when thinkers such as Plato and Aristotle built the philosophical foundations for the subject in civilizations such as Egypt, Greece, and China. Wilhelm Wundt established the first psychology laboratory in the late nineteenth century, ushering in an era of rigorous observation and measurement. As early schools of thought, structuralism and functionalism evolved, delving into the investigation of consciousness and the adaptive functions of behaviour. Psychoanalysis was pioneered by Sigmund Freud, who emphasised the unconscious mind and early experiences.

Watson and Skinner's behaviourist movement switched the emphasis to observable behaviour and conditioning. The mid-twentieth century saw the cognitive revolution, which shifted focus to mental processes. Humanistic psychology, as advocated by Rogers and Maslow, and existential psychology looked at issues of personal growth and meaning. Today, psychology is a dynamic science that encompasses many views such as biological, cognitive, and social psychology, reflecting continual evolution and research.

Practical Applications of Psychology

Psychology has countless practical implications in various areas of life. Psychology is used in a variety of ways, such as:

1. Clinical Practice: Clinical psychologists provide therapy and treatment to those suffering from mental illnesses. They assist patients in dealing with anxiety, sadness, trauma, and other psychological issues.

2. Education: Educational psychologists provide techniques to improve teaching and learning in schools. They can help in the development of effective curriculum, the support of students with learning difficulties, and the resolution of behavioural concerns.

3. Workplace and Organisational Environments: Industrial and organisational psychologists work in businesses and organisations to improve employee productivity, job happiness, and general workplace dynamics. They may conduct assessments, devise training programmes, and coach leaders.

4. Health and Wellness: Health psychologists boost public health by encouraging healthy habits, aiding people in managing chronic conditions, and undertaking health-related research.

5. Law and Criminal Justice: Forensic psychologists operate with the legal system, assessing persons in legal proceedings, providing expert testimony, and doing research on areas such as criminal behaviour and eyewitness testimony.

6. Sports and Performance Enhancement: Sports psychologists help players improve their mental performance, manage stress, and develop psychological skills for sports success.

7. Environmental Sustainability: Environmental psychologists support sustainability initiatives by researching human behaviours and attitudes towards environmental protection. They work on campaigns and activities to promote ecologically mindful behaviours.

8. Mental Health and Well-Being: Psychologists of all disciplines assist people improve their mental health and well-being by providing counselling, psychotherapy, and interventions suited to their personal requirements.

So we see,

Psychology is a broad science that studies the complicated interaction of the human mind and behaviour. Its long history, major theories, research methodologies, subfields, and practical applications make it an important and ever-changing discipline in modern society. Psychologists continue to advance our understanding of human nature, well-being, and the elements that influence our thoughts, feelings, and behaviours. Despite problems and ethical concerns, psychology remains an important instrument for improving the lives of individuals and communities through study, therapy, education, and support. Psychology's relevance in today's world demonstrates its lasting importance as a science of the mind and behaviour.

Pseudosciences: Uncovering the World of Unsubstantiated Beliefs and Practices

Pseudosciences are belief systems or fields of study that claim to be scientific but lack empirical evidence, rely on anecdotal evidence, and frequently embrace unverifiable or supernatural events. Pseudosciences, in contrast to real scientific fields, lack the rigorous procedures, empirical support, and falsifiability that are essential to scientific research. This in-depth examination will go into the world of pseudosciences, examining their characteristics, examples, the reasons people are drawn to them, the potential harm they can cause, and the need of critical thinking in distinguishing them from actual science.

Pseudosciences have various distinguishing features that separate them apart from actual scientific domains. Understanding these features is essential for distinguishing pseudoscientific claims from scientifically grounded knowledge:

1. Astrology: The notion that the placements and movements of celestial bodies such as planets and stars can impact human personality and events is known as astrology. Astrologers generate forecasts and horoscopes based on a person's birth date and the placements of celestial bodies.

2. Palmistry (Chiromancy): Palmistry is the process of divining a person's personality or predicting their destiny by observing the lines, mounts, and features of their hands, especially the palm.

3. Numerology: Numerology is the concept that certain numbers have mystical and divinatory meanings. Names, birthdates, and other numbers are analysed by practitioners to make predictions or provide insights into a person's life.

4. Crystal Healing: According to crystal healing, many crystals and gemstones have therapeutic characteristics and can be utilised to resolve physical, emotional, or spiritual problems. The practice entails the placement or wearing of certain crystals.

5. Dowsing: Dowsing, also known as divining or water witching, is the practice of locating hidden items, water sources, or minerals using equipment such as pendulums or divining rods. It is devoid of scientific evidence and is dependent on the practitioner's interpretation.

6. Phrenology: The concept that the shape and size of the skull can convey information about a person's personality and mental ability is known as phrenology. It has been widely debunked and is now regarded as pseudoscientific.

7. Creationism: Young Earth creationism believes that the Earth is between 6,000 and 10,000 years old and that life, including humans, was created by a divine entity as stated in religious literature. It challenges scientific agreement on evolution and the age of the Earth.

8. Flat Earth Theory: According to the Flat Earth concept, the Earth is flat rather than spherical. This theory runs contrary to millennia of scientific evidence, including studies of the curvature of the Earth.

9. Ufology: The study of unidentified flying objects (UFOs) and the belief in alien visitations is known as ufology. While some UFO sightings go unsolved, the topic is frequently associated with stories of extraterrestrial abductions and government conspiracies.

10. Homoeopathy: Homoeopathy is an alternative medical method that employs highly diluted treatments made from natural components. It is based on the "like cures like" idea and is not supported by scientific evidence.

Myths about Homoeopathy:

1. Myth:

Homoeopathy and herbal medicine are the same thing.

Fact:

Homoeopathy and herbal medicine are two distinct practices. Homoeopathy uses very diluted compounds that may or may not include a molecular trace of the original material, whereas herbal therapy uses plant extracts.

2. Myth:

Homoeopathy is supported by an abundance of scientific data.

Fact:

Homoeopathy is usually regarded as lacking strong scientific proof by the scientific community. Numerous investigations have found no statistically significant difference between homoeopathic therapies and placebos.

3. Myth:

Homoeopathy is capable of curing all diseases.

Fact:

Homoeopathy is not a panacea. Its effectiveness is debated and scientific evidence supporting its efficacy for a variety of illnesses is scarce.

4. Myth:

Homoeopathic medicines are safe because they are highly diluted.

Fact:

Even if homoeopathic treatments are substantially diluted, they can still be dangerous. The dilution process may leave just trace amounts of the original component. but some therapies may not be diluted sufficiently, resulting in potential side effects.

5. Myth:

Homoeopathy works immediately.

Fact:

Homoeopathic treatments are frequently advertised as having rapid effects, although their efficacy is subjective, and any reported improvement could be due to a placebo effect.

Palmistry and Physiognomy

Palmistry and physiognomy are two independent pseudoscientific techniques that involve the interpretation of various physical characteristics to obtain insight into a person's character, personality, or future. While they have certain commonalities, they also have some significant differences:

1. Analysis Focus:

• Palmistry: Palmistry, also known as chiromancy, is the interpretation of a person's hand's lines, mounts, shapes, and features, particularly the palm. It investigates the hand's characteristics and structure.

• Physiognomy: On the other hand, physiognomy focuses on the analysis of facial characteristics and expressions. It examines the shape of the nose, eyes, mouth, and ears, as well as the overall expression of emotions.

2. Physical Characteristics Examined:

• Palmistry: Palmists examine the lines (for example, the heart line, the head line, and the life line), mounts at the base of each finger, and the shapes and features of the hand, fingers, and nails.

• Physiognomy: Practitioners of physiognomy interpret the size, shape, and prominence of facial features such as the nose, eyes, mouth, and ears, as well as the overall proportions of the face. They also examine the individual's facial expressions and behaviours.

3. Cultural Variation:

• Palmistry: Palmistry interpretations can change between countries and traditions, producing in distinct systems and techniques. Indian, Chinese, and Western palmistry, for example, have diverse approaches.

• Physiognomy: Physiognomy exhibits cultural variances, with different cultures interpreting face characteristics and expressions differently. Chinese face reading, for example, differs from Western physiognomy.

4. History and Origins:

• Palmistry: The history of palmistry may be traced back to different ancient civilizations like as India, China, and Greece. It has historical origins in several places of the world.

• Physiognomy: Physiognomy has ancient roots as well, with mentions in ancient Greece and Rome. It has been practiced throughout history in both Western and Eastern cultures.

5. Method of Analysis:

• Palmistry: Palmists use a physical examination to evaluate the lines, mounts, and features of the hand. The physical properties of the palm are used in the analysis.

• Physiognomy: Physiognomists examine an individual's face and expressions during a conversation or interaction to analyse facial traits and expressions. It necessitates a more active evaluation.

6. Principles of Interpretation:

• Palmistry: Palmistry interpretation is founded on the concept that the lines, mounts, and features of the hand are reflective of an individual's character, personality, and future.

• Physiognomy: Physiognomy is based on the notion that an individual's face characteristics and expressions represent their character, personality, and inner attributes.

7. Entertainment and Popularity:

• Palmistry: Palmistry can often be seen as a kind of entertainment at fairs and events. People may choose to have their palms read for entertainment or curiosity.

• Physiognomy: While not as prevalent as a kind of entertainment, certain people may seek face readings for fun or curiosity.

8. Ethical Concerns:

• Palmistry: Ethical issues may arise when people make major life decisions based on palmistry readings that lack scientific validity, potentially leading to exploitation.

• Physiognomy: As with palmistry, ethical issues can arise when people make life-changing decisions based on physiognomy readings that lack factual basis.

In a nutshell,

Palmistry and physiognomy differ principally in their analysis focus, with palmistry focusing on the properties of the hand and physiognomy focusing on facial traits and expressions. Both are pseudoscientific traditions with cultural differences and ethical issues, but they do have certain similarities in terms of subjective interpretation, lack of scientific validity, and ancient significance.

Reasons for Attraction to Pseudosciences

Pseudoscience attracts people for a number of reasons, some of which are very personal and emotionally fraught. Understanding these elements can help explain why people are susceptible to pseudoscientific claims:

1. **Psychological Comfort:** Pseudosciences often give explanations or predictions that provide psychological comfort and control. People may turn to pseudosciences to cope with uncertainty or difficult life circumstances.

2. **Desire for Meaning:** Many pseudosciences promise to give life events meaning or purpose. Individuals drawn to these belief systems may be looking for answers to existential questions or a more profound sense of meaning.

3. **Social and Cultural Factors:** Cultural and social influences can have a considerable impact on whether or not one accepts pseudoscientific thoughts. Beliefs are frequently transmitted through family, culture, or social networks.

4. **Confirmation Bias:** People seek information that validates their existing opinions while discarding or disregarding evidence that opposes those beliefs. Confirmation bias can strengthen pseudoscientific beliefs.

5. **Fear and Uncertainty:** Pseudosciences may prey on people's fears and anxieties, providing remedies or predictions that alleviate their worries. In times of crisis or uncertainty, this might make pseudoscientific ideas more alluring.

6. **Personal Experiences:** Personal stories and testimonials can be great persuading tactics. Individuals who believe they have benefited from a pseudoscience may become proponents of its authenticity.

The Risks of Pseudoscience

While pseudosciences may bring comfort or meet emotional needs for certain people, they can also have negative implications, both personally and societally. Some of the potential consequences of pseudoscience include:

1. **Misleading Health Practices:** Pseudoscientific health therapies can cause people to make unproductive, damaging, or deadly judgements. This includes alternative medicine practices that have not been scientifically validated.

2. **Economic Exploitation:** Many pseudosciences are lucrative businesses. Individuals may spend large sums of money on pseudoscientific services or products that provide no actual benefits.

3. **Delay in Effective Treatment:** Relying on pseudoscientific treatments can delay seeking and getting evidence-based medical or psychiatric care, potentially leading to worsened health issues.

4. **Fostering Mistrust in Science:** Pseudoscientific assertions can weaken public trust in the scientific community, leading to scepticism about real scientific results and consensus on crucial topics.

5. **Pseudoscientific Beliefs and Policy:** When pseudoscientific beliefs affect public policy decisions, the consequences for public health and safety can be disastrous. Vaccine hesitancy, for example, based on pseudoscientific arguments, can result in epidemics of preventable diseases.

6. **Loss of Critical Thinking Abilities:** Adopting pseudoscientific views can degrade critical thinking abilities, making it more difficult for people to differentiate between legitimate information and pseudoscientific assertions.

7. Conflict with Scientific Progress: Investing in pseudoscientific endeavours diverts resources and attention away from actual scientific research and progress.

The Importance of Critical Thinking

To combat the influence of pseudosciences, critical thinking and scientific literacy must be promoted. Critical thinking entails systematically and rationally assessing information, claims, and evidence. Here are some critical thinking principles that can help people evaluate pseudoscientific claims:

1. Evidence-Based Reasoning: Use empirical evidence, scientific research, and peer-reviewed studies to evaluate assertions. Be wary of claims that are based primarily on personal tales or testimonials.

2. Scepticism: Be sceptical of exceptional assertions. Extraordinary claims necessitate extraordinary proof. Before accepting unusual claims as factual, demand rigorous and objective evidence.

3. Falsifiability: Determine whether a claim can be tested and proven wrong. Scientific assertions should be falsifiable, which means that there should be a way to show that they are erroneous.

4. Peer Review: Look for research and statements that have been peer reviewed and scrutinised by subject matter experts. Peer-reviewed studies are more likely to be trustworthy sources of information.

5. Logical Consistency: Look for claims that have internal logical consistency. Claims with logical flaws or contradictions are less likely to be true.

6. Expertise: Take into account the qualifications and expertise of those making specific assertions. Genuine subject matter experts are more likely to deliver accurate information.

7. Corroboration: Look for corroborating evidence from a variety of sources and perspectives. Claims gain credibility when they are independently verified.

8. Distinguishing Science from Pseudoscience: Understand how to differentiate the difference between respectable scientific disciplines and pseudosciences. Recognise the major distinctions in technique and empirical support.

So we see,

Pseudosciences are a diverse universe of unproven claims and unethical behaviours. While they may meet personal needs or give comfort for certain people, they can also pose substantial concerns, such as inaccurate health practices, economic exploitation, and the deterioration of critical thinking skills. To help people identify between pseudoscientific claims and true scientific information, it is vital to develop scientific literacy, scepticism, and critical thinking. By doing so, we can encourage individuals to make informed decisions and contribute to the development of evidence-based practices and policies, eventually increasing individual and societal well-being.

Psychology and Pseudosciences

Pseudosciences and psychology are different fields that deal with human behaviour, cognition, and personality. While psychology is a valid scientific area, pseudosciences are frequently distinguished by unscientific claims and a lack of empirical support. The following are the fundamental distinctions between psychology and pseudoscience:

1. Methodology:

• Psychology: Psychology is founded on empirical information gleaned from systematic research. This includes gathering information, the application of rigorous research procedures, and the analysis of results. Human behaviour is commonly studied using experiments, surveys, observations, and other empirical methods.

• Pseudosciences: These techniques lack empirical proof and do not follow rigorous research methodologies. They frequently base their claims on anecdotal evidence, personal testimonials, or unconfirmed claims.

2. Scientific Method:

• Psychology: Psychologists follow the scientific process, which entails developing hypotheses, conducting tests, and reaching conclusions based on evidence. This methodical technique contributes to the validity and dependability of psychological research.

• Pseudosciences: Pseudoscientific practices are those that do not adhere to the scientific process. They can make claims without developing testable hypotheses, carrying out controlled tests, or submitting their claims to peer review.

3. Theory Development:

• Psychology: Psychologists create theories that serve as frameworks for comprehending human behaviour. Based on fresh information, these theories are constantly evaluated and refined, leading to a better understanding of numerous psychological phenomena.

• Pseudosciences: Pseudosciences often lack established theories backed up by facts from science. They may base their claims on vague or untestable foundations.

4. Peer Review:

• Psychology: In psychology, research findings are subjected to peer review, in which other experts in the field evaluate the technique and outcomes. This procedure contributes to the quality and integrity of psychological research.

• Pseudosciences: Typically, pseudoscientific assertions do not go through thorough peer review in renowned scientific journals. This lack of peer assessment puts into doubt the veracity and dependability of their claims.

5. Ethical Principles:

• Psychology: ethical considerations are an important aspect of psychological research. Researchers must acquire informed consent from subjects, ensure their safety, and maintain confidentiality.

• Pseudosciences: Pseudoscientific practices may not adhere to the same ethical norms as scientific procedures. This can lead to the exploitation of people seeking help or therapy, as well as possibly hazardous pursuits.

6. Credibility and Validity:

• Psychology: Psychology is regarded as a reputable and valid discipline of study due to its emphasis on empirical evidence and scientific principles. It has a large body of research and a solid scientific base.

• Pseudosciences: Pseudosciences are typically viewed with scepticism and chastised for their lack of scientific realism.

They are not supported by empirical evidence, which undermines their legitimacy and scientific validity.

7. Practical Applications:

• Psychology: Psychology has a wide range of practical applications, including clinical therapy, education, business, and sports performance. These applications are based on scientific study and have been shown to be effective.

• Pseudosciences: Pseudosciences often lack scientifically confirmed practical applicability. Their statements do not result in evidence-based initiatives or real-world solutions.

8. Social Implications:

• Psychology: Psychology assists us understand human behaviour and informs evidence-based practice. It is crucial in dealing with mental health issues, improving instructional approaches, and improving workplace dynamics.

• Pseudosciences: Pseudosciences have the potential to mislead the public and propagate unfounded views. People may rely crucial life decisions on pseudoscientific advice, which can have societal and economic ramifications.

Misconceptions concerning the links between psychology and pseudosciences

There are some common misunderstandings or misconceptions about the connections between psychology and pseudosciences. It is critical to address these misunderstandings in order to properly discern between the two sectors. Here are several myths and their associated facts:

1. Myth: Psychology and pseudosciences both investigate the mind and behaviour.

- **Truth:** While both professions deal with human behaviour and cognition, psychology uses empirical research and scientific procedures, whereas pseudosciences often depend on untested assertions and anecdotal evidence. Psychology is distinguished from pseudosciences by its techniques and scientific realism.

2. Myth: Pseudosciences, like psychology, can provide insights and solutions.

- **Truth:** Since pseudosciences lack empirical evidence and scientific validation, their assertions are untrustworthy for understanding or addressing human behaviour and mental processes. As a respectable scientific discipline, psychology provides evidence-based insights and answers.

3. Myth: Some areas of psychology have not been established, making them pseudosciences.

- **Truth:** While there are ongoing debates and areas of research that need to be investigated further, psychology acts within the framework of empirical evidence and scientific scrutiny. This is fundamentally distinct from pseudoscience, which frequently makes untestable or unverifiable assertions.

4. Myth: Psychology and pseudosciences are both concerned with subjective interpretations of human experiences.

- **Truth:** Although both sciences incorporate subjective experiences, psychology tries to analyse and explain these experiences through empirical research and systematic examination. Pseudosciences often provide subjective interpretations that lack empirical foundation.

5. Myth: Certain psychological methods and therapies are pseudoscientific in nature.

• **Truth:** While there are some difficult or unproven techniques in the field of psychology, they do not reflect the entire science. In contrast to pseudosciences, the scientific community and professional organisations endeavour to detect and correct such concerns.

6. Myth: Pseudosciences and psychology can coexist as complimentary approaches.

• **Truth:** Pseudosciences lack scientific legitimacy and have the potential to mislead people, resulting in negative effects. Promoting pseudoscientific views alongside psychology can erode the field's legitimacy and impede evidence-based decision-making.

7. Myth: Both psychology and pseudoscience strive to guide and support individuals.

• **Reality:** Psychology provides individuals looking to understand and enhance their mental health and well-being with evidence-based information and support. Pseudosciences may provide direction, but they lack empirical basis and may not result in dependable or successful answers.

To summarise,

Psychology is a respectable scientific study that provides insights into human behaviour and cognition using empirical evidence, the scientific process, and ethical principles. Pseudosciences, on the other hand, lack these essential characteristics and frequently make unsubstantiated assertions based on subjective interpretations and anecdotal evidence. In our quest to understand human behaviour and cognition, it is crucial to distinguish between the two in order to make informed decisions and promote critical thinking.

The following are the fundamental distinctions between psychology and pseudosciences, provided in tabular form for easy comparison:

Aspect	Psychology	Pseudosciences
Methodology	Employs rigorous research methodologies such as experiments, surveys, and observations to study human behavior.	Often relies on anecdotal evidence and unverified claims, lacking systematic research methodologies.
Scientific Method	Follows the scientific method, which involves formulating testable hypotheses, conducting experiments, and submitting findings to peer review.	Frequently makes assertions without formulating testable hypotheses, conducting controlled experiments, or undergoing peer review.
Theory Development	Grounded in well-established theories, which provide comprehensive frameworks for understanding human behavior.	Often lacks scientifically validated theories, relying on vague or untestable principles to explain claims.
Peer Review	Research findings undergo rigorous peer review by experts in the field before being published in reputable	Claims typically do not undergo peer review by experts, raising questions about their validity and reliability.

	journals.	
Ethical Guidelines	Adheres to ethical guidelines, ensuring informed consent, participant well-being, and confidentiality.	May lack the same ethical standards, potentially leading to exploitation of individuals.
Credibility and Validity	Widely considered a credible and valid field due to empirical evidence, rigorous methods, and scientific foundation.	Often viewed with skepticism and criticized for lack of scientific rigor, lacking empirical support and credibility.
Practical Applications	Has numerous evidence-based practical applications in clinical therapy, education, business, sports, and mental health.	Lacks practical applications that are scientifically validated.
Impact on Society	Contributes to understanding human behavior, influencing policy decisions, and enhancing well-being.	Can mislead the public and promote unfounded beliefs, potentially leading to negative social, economic, and personal consequences.

Psychology and Reverse Psychology

Psychology and reverse psychology are linked concepts, but their objectives and approaches differ. Let's look at all of them separately:

Psychology:

To recap once more, psychology is the scientific study of the human mind and behaviour. It covers a wide range of themes and ways to understanding how people think, feel, and act. Psychologists examine numerous aspects of human behaviour, cognition, and emotions through empirical research, experimentation, and systematic observation. Some significant points concerning psychology are as follows:

1. Scientific Discipline: Psychology is regarded as a competent branch of science. It employs the scientific process, develops testable hypotheses, acquires and analyses evidence, and draws conclusions.

2. Objective Analysis: Psychologists strive to provide objective, evidence-based insights into numerous elements of human life, including memory, perception, emotions, and personality.

3. Therapeutic Applications: Clinical therapy, counselling, educational psychology, sports psychology, and organisational psychology are all areas where psychology can be useful. It assists people in dealing with mental health concerns and improving their overall well-being.

4. Ethical Guidelines: Ethical issues are critical in psychology, guaranteeing the well-being and secrecy of study and therapy participants.

Reverse Psychology:

Reverse psychology is a psychological approach or communication strategy that encourages people to do the opposite of what is suggested in order to affect their behaviour. It entails applying some type of manipulation to obtain a specific result. The following are key characteristics of reverse psychology:

1. Persuasion Technique: Reverse psychology is a type of persuasion in which people are indirectly persuaded to make a certain choice or take a certain action by advocating the opposite.

2. Manipulative Element: It often involves an element of manipulation in order to push someone to act against their own inclinations.

3. Common Application: Reverse psychology is widely used in a variety of contexts, including parenting (e.g., telling a child they can't have dessert to make them want it more), marketing (e.g., advertising limited availability to increase demand), and negotiations (e.g., making an unappealing offer to elicit a more favourable response).

4. Not a Scientific Practice: Although it is based on psychological concepts, reverse psychology is not a scientific activity in the same way that mainstream psychology is. It does not adhere to the scientific approach or seek a better understanding of human behaviour.

Similarities between Psychology and Reverse Psychology

Psychology and reverse psychology are linked in the sense that they both deal with human behaviour and cognition, but their goals and methodologies differ greatly. The following are some similarities between psychology and reverse psychology:

1. Involvement in Human Behaviour: Human behaviour is addressed by both psychology and reverse psychology. As a scientific subject, psychology aims to study and explain human behaviour, whereas reverse psychology use behaviour as a tool to achieve a certain goal.

2. Motivational Understanding: This is a necessary skill for both vocations. Motivation is a fundamental topic of study in psychology, and it investigates why people act the way they do. Understanding what motivates people to act against what is proposed is critical to reverse psychology's efficacy.

3. Communication Techniques: Communication techniques are used in both psychology and reverse psychology. Effective communication is frequently used by psychologists to counsel, guide, and treat clients. In order to persuade or influence behaviour, reverse psychology employs certain communication tactics.

4. Manipulation of Behaviour: Psychology and reverse psychology both strive to affect or manipulate behaviour, while their goals and ethical implications are different. Psychologists may endeavour to assist clients in changing undesirable behaviours, whereas reverse psychology seeks to elicit a specific response by recommending the opposite.

5. Influence on Decision-Making: Both psychology and reverse psychology can have an impact on decision-making. Individuals can make more educated judgements with the help of psychologists. Reverse psychology seeks to influence decision-making by persuading people to act in a specific manner.

Distinctions between Psychology and Reverse Psychology

Psychology and reverse psychology are different concepts with distinct characteristics, objectives, and approaches. Here are the fundamental distinctions between them:

1. Nature and Purpose:

• Psychology is a valid scientific subject that studies human behaviour, cognition, and emotions. Its main goal is to comprehend, explain, and forecast many aspects of human behaviour and brain processes. Empirical study, systematic observation, and the scientific method are used by psychologists to acquire insights into how and why people think, feel, and act the way they do.

• Reverse Psychology: Reverse psychology, on the other hand, is a communication technique or strategy rather than a scientific subject. Its objective is to persuade someone to do the opposite of what is proposed. It is frequently used to elicit a specific outcome or response from a person, such as getting them to comply with a request or make a specific choice.

2. Scientific Rigour:

• Psychology: Psychology is distinguished by its scientific rigour. It takes a methodical and evidence-based approach, conducting experiments, collecting data, and analysing the outcomes to draw conclusions. Psychologists follow ethical principles and strive to deliver objective, well-supported insights into human behaviour.

• Reverse Psychology: Reverse psychology lacks psychology's scientific rigour and empirical foundation. It does not entail systematic research or a dedication to comprehending human behaviour. It instead use communication tactics and manipulation to elicit specified behaviours.

3. Ethical Considerations:

• Psychology: Ethical factors are of the utmost importance in psychology. To safeguard the well-being, confidentiality, and informed consent of research participants and clients, researchers and practitioners in the field follow strict ethical requirements. The ethical principles of psychology emphasise doing no harm and fostering individual well-being.

• Reverse Psychology: In the context of reverse psychology, ethical questions are frequently highlighted. While not necessarily unethical, its manipulative nature can create ethical quandaries, especially when employed to persuade others without their full understanding or agreement.

4. Scope and Application:

• Psychology: Psychology is a vast field with numerous sub-disciplines, including clinical psychology, social psychology, cognitive psychology, and others. It is used to address mental health concerns, enhance well-being, and provide evidence-based recommendations in a variety of settings, including therapy, education, healthcare, and organisational management.

• Reverse Psychology: Reverse psychology is a communication method used to achieve specific goals in specific circumstances such as parenting, marketing, and negotiations. It is not a broad subject of study, but rather a tactic used in certain circumstances.

5. Intent:

• Psychology: The purpose of psychology is to improve our understanding of human behaviour and mental processes, frequently with the goal of increasing individual and communal well-being. It aims to give people knowledge, tools, and therapeutic interventions to help them live healthier and more satisfying lives.

• Reverse Psychology: The goal of reverse psychology is to manipulate or persuade people to act in a certain way, frequently by advocating the inverse. It is a strategy of persuasion intended to elicit a desired response or effect.

In conclusion,

Psychology is a valid scientific subject that investigates and explains human behaviour, cognition, and emotions. It is founded on rigorous research and empirical evidence. In contrast, reverse psychology is a persuasion strategy that encourages people to do the opposite of what is suggested in order to affect their behaviour. It is not a scientific practice and is mostly utilised in practical circumstances to achieve specific results.

Here is a table that compares Psychology and Reverse Psychology:

Aspect	Psychology	Reverse Psychology
Nature and Purpose	Scientific discipline that studies human behavior, cognition, and emotions with the goal of understanding, explaining, and predicting human behavior.	Communication technique or strategy used to influence behavior by encouraging individuals to do the opposite of what is suggested.

Scientific Rigor	Follows scientific method, conducts experiments, and adheres to ethical guidelines.	Lacks scientific rigor and empirical basis.
Ethical Considerations	Adheres to strict ethical guidelines to protect participants' well-being and confidentiality.	Ethical concerns may arise due to the manipulative nature of the technique.
Scope and Application	A broad field with various sub-disciplines (e.g., clinical psychology, social psychology, etc.) and applied in diverse settings, such as therapy, education, healthcare, and more.	Applied in specific contexts, such as parenting, marketing, and negotiations, to achieve specific outcomes.
Intent	Intent is to increase understanding of human behavior, promote well-being,	Intent is to persuade or manipulate behavior by suggesting the opposite.

Final Thoughts

The complex tapestry of human existence weaves together threads of consciousness, subconsciousness, societal standards, and the never-ending desire of understanding. As we navigate the intricacies of our minds and communities, it becomes clear that the path to self-awareness is not a linear one, but rather a constant investigation distinguished by humility and curiosity.

While education is a valuable tool for fostering critical thinking, it should be accompanied by an acknowledgement of the immense unknown that exists beyond the bounds of certainty. The interaction between the conscious and subconscious minds highlights the richness of our identities, encouraging us to explore the depths of our thoughts and motivations with an open heart and mind.

A more sophisticated strategy is needed to address the challenges of psychological wellness, global issues, and societal norms beyond the surface level of unflinching certainty. Empathy, understanding, and a collective reckoning with conventional wisdom become essential as we address the contradictions inherent in our human experience.

In light of these complexity, the search of self-awareness and society understanding necessitates a shift away from simplistic narratives and a willingness to accept the fluidity of truths. Humankind's path to enlightenment must be distinguished by a continuous dedication to unravelling the mysteries, admitting the limitations of our existing understanding, and cultivating an openness to the ever-changing nature of our being.

Lastly, it is only through this humble recognition of our own fallibility and real curiosity about the perplexing nature of humanity that we can expect to promote a greater understanding of ourselves and the society we live in, thereby contributing to a more compassionate and complex world.